FROM
BROKE, BUSTED AND DISGUSTED
TO A
MILLION DOLLARS
A YEAR

THE **CEDRIC PENN** STORY

From Broke, Busted and Disgusted
To A Million Dollars A Year- The Cedric Penn Story
Copyright © 2010
Cedric D. Penn Enterprises

ALL RIGHTS RESERVED

No portion of this publication may be reproduced, stored in any electronic system, or transmitted in any form or by any means, electronic, mechanical, photocopy, recording or otherwise without written permission from the author. Brief quotations may be used in literary reviews.

ISBN: 978-0-9828360-0-2

ISBN: 978-0-9828360-1-9 Hard Cover

Published By:

Cedric D. Penn Enterprises

4620 Morton Road

Alpharetta, Georgia 30022

Email: ContactCedric@TheCedricPennStory.com

www.FromBrokeBustedDisgusted.com
www.TheCedricPennStory.com
www.CedricDewaynePenn.com

First Run: July 2010

Printed in the United States of America

Dedicated In Honor of:

Laura Ann McGee Clemons & Oscar "Thunder" Clemons, Sr.,
Oscar "Big O" Clemons, Jr. & Elaine Penn

John De Simone & Tony Iaconni

Brian Thomas, Richard Woods & Wayne Lancaster

Special Thanks To:

Catherine Travis Penn, Tina Danford Penn,

Cedric D. Penn, Jr., Venetra Penn

& Sierra Jade Brown

Charles Penn, Sharon Penn, Mark Penn, Douglas Penn,

Jeffrey Penn, Kirk Penn, My Nieces, Nephews & Cousins

Darlene "Cookie" Danford, Eck Knisley, Judge Cicchetti, Herb Mitchell, Sr., Bill Romanowski, Dave Gaskill, Dave Roberts, Mrs. Howard, Bruce Taylor, Brent "Batman" Jones, George "Icky" Green, Derek 'D.K.' Green, Kevin Holley, Kevin Elko, Jerry "Rhino" Clark, Teresa Howell, Lillie Mae Bates, Joe Tiller, Jaimie Stagesin, Jenny Stagesin & The Late John Stagesin, Bill & Debbie Fields, Tracy Hayes and Lonnie Robinson

TABLE OF CONTENTS

Foreword:	Bill "Romo" Romanowski	1
Prologue:	Faith	5
Chapter 1:	Rudimentary Beginnings	15
Chapter 2:	Highly Favored	39
Chapter 3:	On The Line	53
Chapter 4:	After The Draft	71
Chapter 5:	Wind Beneath My Wings	84
Chapter 6:	Success Is A Decision	101
Chapter 7:	It's Better To Watch A Leader Than Listen To One	115
Chapter 8:	The Power of Culture	128
Chapter 9:	Finalé Revealed	139

Foreword

After 16 years in the NFL and four Super Bowl Championships, I hope that I can share with you some of my humble understanding of what it takes to be successful and reach your goals. After leaving football for the world of business, my eyes were opened to the immense challenges that we all face each and every day, whether it is paying the bills, getting fit, or just boosting your self-confidence.

Like everyone else on this planet, I have made my fair share of mistakes. But I am proud of the tenacity with which I have lived my life. After all this, I truly believe that life is the biggest Super Bowl ever and the world is your playing field.
Whether you are running your own business, raising your children, striving as an athlete, or pursuing your education, it takes character, determination, tenacity, leadership, "coachability," and above all, an unstoppable will to win to be successful.

Most people have these traits inside them but have not learned to maximize them to their fullest potential. After reading Cedric's book, you will learn to fully capitalize on these traits, as well as develop your own natural strengths to reach your goals.

"From Broke, Busted and Disgusted To A Million Dollars A Year- The Cedric Penn Story" does more than inspire. Penn outlines a step by step plan to turn your inspiration into reality. He gives you the tools you need to reach your own definition of success.

I wish you all the best in your pursuit of excellence and I truly hope you take the material in this book to heart so that you can develop into your own World Champion.

Bill Romanowski

"I Will Continue To Do Whatever I Have To Do To

Get What I Want.

Until I Get My Family Where I Want Them To Be,

I Will Until…."

Prologue

◆ *Faith*

As I lay face down on the pavement, I could hear five or six cars pass me by. I began to recite Psalm 23:

"The LORD is my shepherd; I shall not want.

He maketh me to lie down in green pastures: he leadeth me beside the still waters.

He restoreth my soul: he leadeth me in the paths of righteousness for his name's sake.

Yea, though I walk through the valley of the shadow of death, I will fear no evil: for thou art with me; thy rod and thy staff they comfort me.

Thou preparest a table before me in the presence of mine enemies: thou anointest my head with oil; my cup runneth over.

Surely goodness and mercy shall follow me all the days of my life: and I will dwell in the house of the LORD for ever."

I got through the passages once, and then began again. The second time towards the end, I stopped and— I could not feel my legs. It was at that point I pleaded: *God, if you are going to take me, please take me in front of my family; don't let me die on the side of the road.* I heard a voice say, "I'm not going to let you die" and it kind of startled me. I thought someone was standing behind me talking, so I tried to roll over but, there wasn't anyone. The cars were going by fast and— I knew that the voice I heard was *God*. Before He spoke to me, I was in pain. Afterwards, I was no longer.

—I lay helpless, unable to move and at the mercy of only God, as His grace would be the only way my life would be spared—

And I undoubtedly knew the reason for the accident. Events began to replay like flashing scenes from a movie: my family, childhood, church, little league, the truck accident, college, the NFL, the projects, drugs, politics, business deals, money, death, cars, women, extortion and again, my family. Except, it wasn't at all a movie that I had ever stopped to watch— *that is*, until this very moment as I lay there looking at my life, my reality. Remaining conscious the entire time, I knew that just a few moments earlier I had been in Gwinnett County; right outside of Atlanta, Georgia riding my Harley Davidson down Lawrenceville Highway at Ronald Regan Parkway. I was enjoying the ride while listening to my favorite R & B group, *The Isley Brothers*. It was Tuesday, December 16th, 2008; just nine days before Christmas. As I proceeded through the intersection, a black truck disregards the light as it came through striking me, and throwing my body into the air. The driver never got out to see if I was alive. Neither did the passersby that followed. I was left on the side of the road alone and critically injured.

A moment or so later, an unexpected touch to my neck caused me to jump; which in turn, startled what would be a man checking for my pulse. I don't believe he thought that I was alive. He asked my name and if I knew where I was. Due to the severity of my injuries I could not see him but responded, 'Cedric Penn, I was on my bike.' The male voice then inquired as to whether I had a phone on me. I told him to look in my right pocket. I could feel him move my body to get to the phone. I said, just press number one; my number one is my Mom. Following just as I instructed, the male voice on my end asked, "Is this Cedric Penn's mother?" I could hear my mother's voice coming through the speaker of the phone as she responded, "who is this? Yes, that's my baby!" At forty-one years old, I was still her baby. I told the still unidentified man to put the phone down by my mouth. As I called out her name she asked, "Wayne, is that you?" Of my family and childhood friends; most all called me Wayne —short for my middle name 'Dewayne'— able to respond I said, 'yeah Mom, I was in a bad motorcycle accident.' Immediately panicking, she frantically cried out to the house for help, "Your brother is hurt, your brother is hurt" and yelling,

"Is my baby dead?" The male voice responded with urgency, "no, he is not dead, but he *is* seriously injured." I remember the last thing I said was, 'Mom just get down here; I'm hurt real bad, just get down here.' Assuring me as my Mother always would, she replied "baby, I'll get there as quickly as I can," as the faint sound of blaring sirens began coming from a distance. Back at home, my wife and I had a disagreement, an argument. I left out on the ride without saying anything to her— or my children, not even goodbye. Now here I am lying on the ground not knowing if I will ever again have the opportunity to see their faces, or if it is that time, say goodbye and tell them I love you.

Paramedics delivered me to the Gwinnett County Medical Center Trauma Unit at two forty-seven p.m. I was in critical condition, yet still conscious as the team of doctors ran my body through the MRI machine, twice. I remember hearing the female voices call out all of the injuries to my body and everything that was going to have to be repaired, "crushed pelvis, twenty-three fractures in right arm, crushed right elbow, broken left wrist, broken right wrist, crushed nasal, numerous facial fractures, jawbone bone loss, eight teeth knocked out..." as the voices continued calling out my other fractures and injuries, all I knew was that I was in excruciating pain from my arm as I lay on the hospital gurney. Then I heard the familiar voice of my son, Cedric, Jr. call out for me— from somewhere in that emergency room. It was followed by high pitched yells from Venetra and Tina. God was doing just as He had promised out on Lawrenceville Highway; He was not going to let me die. As they rushed me into what would be eighteen hours of surgery, I told my daughter, 'you will always be daddy's little girl.' Following surgery, I remained in a coma for two more days. My true loved ones stepped up and showed their brilliant colors with genuine thoughts and prayers, well-wishings, calls, cards, visits and offerings of "whatever I can do." The haters showed up, too—and in full force.

—It is ultimately in your hour of need that you learn who and where your true support comes from; who is covering your back to protect you and who is covering your back, just waiting for the perfect opportunity to stab you. I believe that everything happens in life the way it is meant. The harder and more challenging events are caused for you to

reassess your life; to help put it all in perspective—

Literally at the exact hour that I was fighting for my life, board meetings were strategically being scheduled in different parts of the country, with the sole agenda to disintegrate my position within and oust me out of the company that I was a part of; the company that I, along with its President, Braden Seward, help build— Zielar International. Unbeknownst to the independent distributor base of the company, problems separate from the controversial compensation plan change, had begun to ensue behind closed doors. Corporate political tension and competition surmounted as did the financial pressures, causing unrest amongst the already unsound executive board members under the leadership of company CEO, Karl Braselton.

And little did I know that the events leading up to, and just after this accident, were only prelude of that which was yet to come over the next eighteen months. Members of my own organization- The Diamond Network, people that my family and I had regarded as friends and helped over the years; even the woman, with whom I placed my trust and formed a close and intimate relationship with would all soon turn on me in exchange for a payoff check from Zielar.

Chapter 1

♦ *Family*

RUDIMENTARY BEGINNINGS

Even before my birth, my family had always been very close-niched. My parents, Catherine Travis Penn and Oscar "Big O" Clemons, Jr. were initially introduced at the home of their mutual friend, Diane King. Diane and my Mother lived in the same apartment complex and my Father, along with his friend, had come over for a social gathering. My parents didn't exactly hit it off in the beginning; it seems my Father had a genuine interest in my Mother, but because of his *"cocky and loud"* persona, she was a little apprehensive. She often recalls how he enjoyed teasing her and jokingly ordering "hey girl, come here!" The two, however, shared a commonality of being only children. Because my maternal Grandmother, Isabelle "Belle" Hershey, passed away when my Mother was eight and my maternal Grandfather, Charles Travis, left shortly thereafter— not to return until my Mother was fourteen, she was raised by her maternal Aunt Mary Lee Dixon. My Father on the other hand, was raised— through his teenage years, in a home with both of his parents, Laura Ann McGee and Oscar "Thunder" Clemons, Sr., until my Grandfather suffered a stroke and passed away at the age of fifty-seven. So that he could help to support my Grandmother and cover the household expenses, my Father enlisted in the service, under the military branch of the Army and was stationed at Fort Bragg in North Carolina where he was a Medic. Strong work ethics was an inherited trait instilled by my Grandparents; both of whom were no-nonsense when it came down to doing what you are supposed to do. My Grandfather, a Mason, was the first African-American to become Supervisor in the coal mines of rural Pennsylvania. Though he stood only about five feet seven inches tall, it was said that he did not take *shit* from anyone; instead, taking pride in protecting and providing for his family. It was his regular routine after coming out of the mines to go home, wash up and change into a *slick* suit for the remainder of the day. As it was, they were the first African-American household in their area to own a television set and my Father would charge his friends a nickel each to come over and watch it. Oscar, Sr. hailed from North Carolina (Stokes County), right outside of Winston-Salem, but he met my Grandmother after going up north to look for work. She herself an Eastern Star, had migrated from Natchez, Mississippi.

At the time that my parents met, they both had children from previous relationships. My Father had a son, Kevin and a daughter, Laura Ann (named for my Grandmother) while my mother had two girls and five boys; Elaine, Charles "Chuck", Mark, Douglas, Sharon, Jeffrey and Kirk "Big." She held a part-time position at Penn State College, in the head office, for the Upward-Bound program. After the service, my Father followed his own father's footsteps, going on to become a second generation coal miner and then a steel mill worker. Later in life, my Father would be sworn in as a Constable for the State of Pennsylvania; an achievement that my Mother regards as one of her most memorable moments shared with my Father. Early in their courtship, my parents made the decision to align as a family unit. They moved their new family to Nine-Fifteen Second Street in Brownsville, a small township situated in southwestern Pennsylvania, and the source from where all my memories began. Our home set atop a hill in a wooded and very diverse, yet close community. It was a three story, four floor house with five bedrooms. Brownsville has always been shallowly populated, having approximately six thousand residents of which, roughly two thirds are children. Our family was one of few African-American households in the neighborhood with my Father being —as his own was— an incredible provider. The community did not distinguish between ethnic backgrounds as everyone was treated the same where we lived. Over the years, both of my parents became pillars as the 'Penn' family name was— and still is, well respected and highly regarded in Brownsville's community.

Catherine Travis Penn, my mother, was forty-three years old at the time, and the oldest woman giving birth in the Brownsville General Hospital Maternity Ward on August 7, 1966. Having suffered two miscarriages after her pregnancy with me (both boys), I was meant to be her last child. Because of her age, doctors advised her not to continue the pregnancy, as the risk of possible mental and physical impairments would increase. However, firmly grounded in her decision, my Mother opted otherwise and miraculously she delivered me naturally, a healthy fourteen pound boy that— with my Father, they named Cedric Dewayne Penn. Unexpectedly and after giving birth to me, she hemorrhaged severely and her heart stopped. As the hospital signaled code ninety-nine (commonly referred to as *code blue*), my Mother went into full cardiac arrest; experiencing a supernatural event she would later be able to recall. It was after successful resuscitation, that she explained her experience being drawn towards a white light in a place where she could hear everyone in the room talking, but she herself, was unable to speak. And it was at that place, that she emphatically states she saw the face of *God*. Personally, I feel as though my life, since the very beginning, has been against the odds and —spiritually speaking— that I may be a baby of an angel. In many ways, future events seemingly reveal my Mother to be my *Guardian Angel*. The same day of my birth, my Step-Grandmother— a spiritualist, came to visit my Mother in the hospital and proclaimed that I was going to be "a great man," that my mother was "going to be very proud of me" and that I was "going to be a rich man."

As far back as I can remember our home was one encompassed by love, respect, values, structure, discipline and of course, unity. There was a great variance in our ages and Elaine, the eldest of us, was already grown, married and out of the house when I was born. She took loving care of me, though. Over the years, our close bond would always remain. From bathings and sittings to feedings and changings, Elaine took over all of the responsibilities calling me *her baby*. Her own son, Kirk (whom we call "Little Kirk" for being named after our brother) was born just eight months after me and our relationship would grow to be one more-so as brothers rather than uncle and nephew. Much of my early years were also spent with my paternal Grandmother, Laura Ann, who lived about three miles away from us. I look just like her. Though I was her only biological Grandson, she and my Grandfather had adopted a daughter, Virginia (Aunt Deanie) whom had three sons of her own; Rudy, Johnny and Isaac. My Grandmother loved all of her Grandsons the same. As young boys and even throughout our lives, my cousins and I have always been very close. Like my own Mother, my Grandmother was very strict, but we had a wonderful relationship and a special bond. The first Easter Sunday that I can remember, she bought me a suit and took me to church where I said my first recitation piece during the morning program. And she would always bake me fresh bread and make apple butter— every day. How I loved to wake up to the smell of her home cooking and as I got older, she would send me on runs to the store. No matter how much money I would ask her for in return, my options were a quarter or some banana pudding; that's it— no more, no less. I always chose the quarter because you could get lots of penny candies for it. My favorites were jawbreakers, fireballs and the round caramel chews with the white cream in the middle. My Grandmother had always been a very meticulous person. She kept her house, just-so and there were rules. One rule being that the kitchen closed at six p.m. and another, that if you pee'd in her bed, you would get a 'whooping.' A no-nonsense Christian woman, very much involved in the church and Eastern Stars organizations, she was for sure, a real woman whom I loved dearly and highly respected, as well.

Life in the Penn home was relatively similar to that of other middle-class families, I presume. My Father was the *'Head of the Household'* and my Mother was the *'Head Sergeant In Charge of Operations.'* As such, that meant he went out and made the money and she made sure everything that needed to be, with regards to the family and the household, was handled. She was nicknamed *Sergeant Carter* around the house and we were definitely fearful of not doing what we were supposed to, what was expected from us, as she did not fool around when it came to rules and discipline. *Sergeant Carter* ran a tight ship and kept close range making sure that all eight of her *crew members* stayed in line. All of the older siblings had chores; from cleaning to ironing, whatever it was, it had to be done before you could leave the house. Her curfew and disciplinary policies were streamlined, too. Be home by eleven-fifteen p.m., you get one warning and if no one fesses up to her unanswered question of mischief, line em' up, everybody's getting it. Those were the rules and we knew them well. Make no mistake, though, we weren't angels. Around the house, my brother, Mark and my sister, Sharon always fought like cats and dogs over one thing or ten others. And if there had been video cameras hidden, the footage would have proved to be great entertainment. For instance, the holiday— I believe it was *Thanksgiving*; when we had company over, played all day and had a great time. At the end of the night though, the house was a mess and my Mother found orange peels inside the fireplace. She came to me and asked, "Who put those orange peels in that fireplace?" Thinking to myself, why did she have to ask me? I stumbled on my words replying, 'I-I d-don't how they got there. Somebody put em' in there'. That was a line em' up moment. Mom figured her method was a "no-fail" one. Either way, she would get to the culprit. But there were some other instances that got past her, like whenever we had beans for dinner. I hated beans and would either lower them under the table to our German Sheppard, *Puddles* or wrap them into a napkin, saving them to give him during the nightly car drive he would require before going to sleep— Puddles, that is.

In every value and lesson that my Mother planned

to instill into her children, she did everything within her power to make sure that her missions were successful. Incessantly sitting us down, she would beat into our heads the importance of sticking together and looking out for one another, no matter what. And she drilled into us, the notion of working hard and getting our education, especially the boys, whom my Mother insisted on achieving college degrees. To this day, despite the fact that we are all grown —college graduates— with grown children of our own, she still drills the importance of us sticking together as a family. It has not changed, though if it ever did, that would be our cue to worry.

My brothers, sisters and I were all close, but Big and I shared bedrooms since we were closest in age, and we ran together the most. Sports were a major influence in our household, but also within our local community. My brothers were all involved in at least one area of sports or another, which is probably why I got involved so early in life. Jeff, my middle brother, was highly competitive in basketball while my eldest brother Chuck was very much focused on baseball, though he played football, too. In fact, my first true love in sports is baseball. Dad first signed me up into little league when I was six, although the minimum age requirement was eight. I wanted to play and because of my size, weight, and oh yes, his pen changing the year on my birth certificate, I was in the league pitching and playing first base in no time. Chuck was a great supporter, too. He bought me my first baseball, glove and bat during a visit home from college. The lessons and discipline that I learned so early on from coaches —like Dave Gaskill, who taught me how to be a student of Baseball. He took it from having fun to having and making sense. And Tony Iacconi, who would always tell me, even through the years and until his passing in 2010, that I was the best player he ever coached; Charlie Smith (who was also a *father figure* to me) — were intricate keys to my success in sports as a child and also my future successes in life and business.

After entering kindergarten at Cox-Donahey Elementary the same year that I began little league, I got into basketball and football, as well. Going to school was a change, but it was fun. Big and I rode the school bus together, along with our friends from the neighborhood which was about ten miles away from the school. For us, everything was about outdoor activities; sports, mud bikes, and playing— that was our outlet. It also became my scapegoat from doing chores. I quickly learned to keep myself actively involved in sports so that come first thing Saturday mornings when the chore list was handed out, I was already out of the house and off to practice. Dad was a huge sports fan; therefore he always supported all of his boys' involvement. Often times, I would go along with him to watch my brother Kevin play during his football games. My Father worked hard and prided himself in making sure that he was able to provide everything that his family needed and wanted, the same way my Grandfather had done when my Dad was growing up. On his way home from work, be it the steel mills, coal mines or serving warrants— all of which he did, he would always stop off first and pick us up something, never walking through the front door without a goodie bag for us. Whether it'd be a pie, ice cream, cookies or candy, he always made sure that he had something. And I don't know why it was, but he would return home with his lunch in its pail, still intact; so I would make sure to follow behind after he sat it on the counter and finish it up.

Mount Lebanon Baptist Church was a place that I looked forward to attending each week with my family; it was where we all came together. Many of our neighborhood and school friends attended, as well, and we all participated together in the church's youth choir and bible study groups. We also would get in trouble together after going across the street to the neighborhood store, Shin's, to buy candy and afterwards leaving the wrappers in the pews. It wasn't the pastor, whom we called "Rev", that would get us, but whichever pair of *motherly* eyes spotted the wrappers first. I have so many faith rooted seeds and memories that were planted because of the early religious teachings at the church. Mrs. Sandra McCain, then a member of the church, now the Pastor of Mount

Lebanon, was the first lady that I looked up to from a biblical perspective. To me, she always seemed to be such a pure and pristine woman of *God*. There was just something about her; she taught me values and was very instrumental in teaching me to read the Bible. And also Mrs. Howard who, to this day, does not look like she ages one bit. She is an incredible Christian lady; an ambassador for Christ. It has always seemed like she has a serious *direct connect* to God. Whatever she prays for, He delivers. When I was involved in the motorcycle accident, she prayed for me around the clock. Thinking back, as teenagers we looked forward to going over to her house each week for youth Bible study. She would allow us to hang out a little while first before we got started, and later, she would lead us in prayer and worship. Mrs. Phips, another church member, was also active in my life, as she taught me how to play the piano.

For me, biblical teaching was not contained to church. It was my school bus driver, Sunny, that gifted me my first pocket Bible. It was a very nice; burgundy in color, and although he did not attend Mount Lebanon, the two of us often sat and discussed the scriptures. In fact, he was the first guy with whom I discussed the Bible.

Although the church had its regular schedule and weekly activities, the influence of the *Pittsburgh Steelers* was infectious and extended throughout our community as everything within it would shut down. And if they were scheduled to play during church hours, it was my Mother who would be sure to inform the Pastor that "we're not going to be here all day." Big Sunday dinners were a must in our home. After service, everyone would come over to our house where my Mother would cook delectable meals and my Father would *throw down* on the open-barrel bar-b-que grill in the backyard, making his famous ribs accented with his special secret sauce.

My memories of elementary school are pretty traditional. In the third grade I befriended a classmate, Tom Burns. The two of us became the best of friends. We hung out, played sports, did school projects and even rode the school bus together. But it was in fourth grade that I developed a great interest in music and instruments; joining the stage band. I learned and went on to play the clarinet, saxophone, drums and also the guitar for the remaining two elementary and entire three middle school years. My family always supported any interests I had. However, the more advanced I became in learning the instruments, the more concerned my Father was about my involvement in sports. He thought I may opt for the band over football and baseball, but in my mind that was never going to happen because I loved sports entirely too much. Upon graduating from the sixth grade, I learned that my best friend Tom and his family were relocating to Florida, which really disappointed me. And though all of my other friends would matriculate with me to Red Stone Middle School, at the time he was my closest buddy.

It was somewhat of an adjustment changing schools. Obviously the campus was larger as five area elementary schools fed into it, but the structure and my focus remained the same, pretty much. Dad had already taught me how to drive and would allow me to take myself to practice or run an errand for my Mother. Although I had a running crew; Brian Thomas, William "Snooks" Thomas, Richard Woods and Mike Isaac, if I wasn't at school, practice or Bible study, I would be at home, outside. We didn't just arbitrarily hang out the way kids do now-a-days, or at least, that was not how it went in our home. My Mother kept a tab as to who we associated with. If my parents did not know our friends *and* their parents, it was not happening. So in the eighth grade, when I had my first girlfriend, Terri Ashburn, it was okay because her sister and my sister were best friends. Although we didn't go to the same school, I would see her whenever I went over to Elaine's house. That was also the year that I broke my leg while playing ball. I remember going home and saying, 'Dad, my leg really hurts' and him telling me that I "would be alright." He could be hard, but it was for the right reasons and it was also those teachings that, later on in life, I would be able to understand and appreciate. He made me wait three days before taking me to the doctor. The broken leg kept me from playing ball, but did not completely cut off my fun. Herb Mitchell, Sr., the Father of one of friends, owned a place called *The Game Room*. As it offered an array of activities; various video arcade games and a pool table, playing *Asteroids* while eating *Slim Jims*, was a favorite past-time of mine.

Many weekends Dad would take us out, just driving. I remember that he would take us through these elite neighborhoods in the Malden area where I was fascinated by the luxurious homes and lifestyles. Very much intrigued as to how they attained it, I would blatantly ask, 'Dad, how do these people have all of this stuff?' Back then, if you saw a Mercedes, it was a big deal and these homes would have two parked in their driveway. I would sit there trying to figure out how they do it— how can they afford all of this, and my Dad would say, "son they own businesses." Of course, that wasn't enough information for me so I'd follow-up with, 'well what kind of businesses do they own?' Again he would respond, "they-own-businesses." So I'd sit there thinking to myself, okay they live over here, have money and own businesses and we live over there and have jobs. How does that work? What do I have to do to get over here? It seemed like those families were just going through life with no stress; playing with their children who had everything from motorcycles to quads, I mean— you name it and they had it. Don't get me wrong, for an African-American child, I had a lot, too and one of my best friend's Father was the President Judge, so he had a big house, but these homes in Malden just seemed to be massive and their lifestyles completely opposite of ours.

Chapter 2

♦ *Family*

HIGHLY FAVORED

It was a couple of nights before *Grid Iron Night* and we were supposed to go to a party. There were three of us in the Ford pick-up truck that my buddy Richard was driving. Mike was in the middle and I was seated on the passenger side. It was sometime between ten thirty and ten forty-five at night, but because my Mother said that I "better be home by eleven-fifteen," I instead had them drop me off first. I went into the house and went to bed, as usual. Around six o'clock the next morning, I awoke to the sound of my parents banging on my door followed by my Mothers yell, "he's in the bed asleep." I got up and went downstairs where Pennsylvania State Troopers were standing in our living room. One of the officers said, "Son we've been looking for you all night." Apparently, about twelve minutes after Richard and Mike dropped me off, they hit a tree and the truck exploded; throwing Mike from it and trapping Richard who— lost his life in the fire. When the State Troopers got to Mike, he was going in and out of consciousness, but kept asking "where's Wayne?" So, they spent the night searching for me out in the woods thinking that I had been involved in the accident, as well. I was fifteen years old at the time. That was definitely a changing point; the first life altering experience and the first time that discipline and family values directly impacted my life. It was my Mom who saved me because I had to get back home to *Sargent Carter*. She was adamant about my being home by eleven fifteen and that's what I had to do.

I returned to my bedroom and looked out my window where I could see Richard's house across the way. As family members began arriving at his home, I knew that the news was true. It had only been Richard and his three younger sisters; Toni, La Weeta and Lorraine along with their Mother, Ms. Bunny, whom was also friends with my Father. Dad helped out in covering Richard's final expenses. From that point forward, I became much more focused on school and sports. Not that my concentration had ever been redirected, but I was just focused *now* more than ever; working harder, trying to do and be the best that I could.

There had been two community high schools; Red Stone High and Brownsville High. Red Stone always had an incredible football program and Brownsville's was the opposite. However, in the late sixties, the two schools merged together forming Brownsville Area High School and everyone was excited about the new football team, thinking it would be a *powerhouse,* but that was not the case. However, it was between my freshman and sophomore school years that we completely changed the tradition of the school; going from losing, to becoming the first winning season for Brownsville in about twenty years. Being one of the youngest on the *varsity* team, the coaches threw me out there and really pushed me, which was a good thing because by my time that I reached my junior year, my quarterback sacks were —twenty three— being one of top numbers in the state of Pennsylvania for a junior. The coaches had a huge impact on my development; suffice to say that I had five of the most influential coaches during those highs school years— John De Simone and Lou De Simon; two brothers whom had also went to school with my Dad, Willie Vasiloff— who, in addition to being one of the football coaches, was also the school's *Principal*, Don De Fino and Ray Ebbert. Aside from sports, K.W.K. Productions —standing for the abbreviation of our names— was formed by my brother Big, my nephew Little Kirk and I. Hip-hop group Run DMC, now legendary pioneer icons, had not long before come out and they were a huge force around the world. Like everyone else, we had the big gold rope chains, Kangol hats and Adidas sneakers and jackets. My Dad bought us a turntable, so we would go around deejaying parties through K.W.K. Productions. In my junior and senior years, I really tightened up on my grades and *crushed it*. Never a dumb guy in school, before I just had only done as much as I needed to in order to get through, but I knew that if I wanted to go to a big school and play, my grades and S.A.T. scores would have to be up. They would not give you thousands of dollars in scholarships if your S.A.T. scores were low. In addition, *Proposition 48* was implemented, and though somewhat controversial, it said that if you did not receive a particular S.A.T. score minimum, you would be ineligible to play in college games; having to sit out on the bench. Schools were not going to pay anybody to sit out. The coaches would remind us of this, drilling it into our heads every day. So, I did what I had to in the classroom; of my favorite subjects, *Business Law*. It is kind of funny when you think about it, small town Brownsville; coal mines, steel mills and drugs, but we had business law classes in high school.

On the field, I was a star athlete; equally strong in both baseball and football. Coaches, recruiters and schools began taking notice. The turnout at the games was phenomenal and of course, my family would always come out to support me. The

Milwaukee Brewers brought me down to tryout with them and ended up offering me a contract. Decisions were upon me as now I had to decide if I wanted to deviate from college and sign a contract in baseball or wait it out and earn the scholarships that I had been working so hard for, since I was a child. Baseball was my first love, but that would mean the end of my football career. Was I ready for that? You hear so many stories about people playing in the minor league for fifteen or twenty years, never making it into the majors. I declined the offer. In hindsight, that was a big mistake because I allowed fear to influence my decision. Upon returning home, I began redirecting my focus mainly on football. My Father and brother Doug would come to the games and get so caught up in the atmosphere that they would be out in the stands taking bets. As the sports seasons progressed and changed, so did my athletic capability. Like clockwork, I would come home and the two of them would just rip my game apart, as if I had not done anything at all; dissecting the game play-by-play telling me everything that I did wrong. Even if I had a great game, I would dread coming home and walking through the door because I knew that they were on the other side just waiting on me and it was coming. They would do the same thing after my practices, too. It was crazy, but in a great way because it was their way of keeping me humble; trying to help mold me into the best player. Our games were like wars. The schools literally ceased the night games, opting for afternoon games because of it. In a game against Bethlehem Center, my teammate and friend Curtis Brown was running the ball when Beth Center's player, Jimmy Havilesko, hit him; resulting in a broken neck and leaving himself temporarily paralyzed. It was a freak accident, but just goes to show how intense our games could get. Controversy escalated and continued for months between the two schools as Beth Center students said we cheered when Jimmy got hurt, which was not true. We made it to the second or third round of the state play-offs during my senior year, all the while playing in six inches of snow; ultimately loosing eight to seven because our quarterback decides to take a safety instead of throwing the ball away. I was mad for an entire year about that one. Every time I thought about it, I got mad all over again. More and more agencies inquired about me; from scouts to schools; agents to coaches, they knew of me more than I even realized. One weekend, I sat at home in the living room watching *ESPN's Big Ten Conference* on television. Purdue University was playing in a game that absolutely captivated me. As I watched from the couch, I remember silently praying, *God...*

if you could give me an opportunity to go there... At the time, I was getting letters and phone calls from different universities, but nothing ever from Purdue.

All of my siblings were grown and pretty much gone. The dynamics in the household had changed and because my parents were going through their own personal relationship issues; rapid changes continued. I didn't want to be put in the middle of what was taking place with them and I refused to take sides. Dad was my best friend. Emotionally, I tried to separate myself while still holding on to my relationship with each of them respectfully, focusing past graduation, just going off to a big college, preferably one of my choice, to play ball.

I received a random phone call at home one evening from Mr. Nichols, the head of maintenance at my school. He and I didn't have any association outside of school, so it was a little surprising when he called and even more so when he went on to ask if I was "planning on attending school the following day?" He continued, "If you are planning on not coming to school tomorrow, you might want to make sure you are here because I just received a phone call from a coach and he is trying to make sure that you are going to be in school tomorrow." Well, that wasn't a big deal because coaches would come to the school all the time. Sure enough the next day during homeroom, immediately following the morning announcements, Principal Vasiloff — who is also one of my coaches— walks into the classroom and directly up to me stating, "Purdue is down in the office. They want to see you." Thinking out loud to myself, as well as responding to him, 'I've never received anything from Purdue, what do they want with me?' I go down to the office and there is a blonde haired gentleman sitting in the room. He introduces himself as Bill Doba, going on to say that he had "heard a lot of great things about me" and asked if I would "be interested in coming out to take a look at the school." Still puzzled, I hesitantly questioned how he had heard about me and he began telling me that when went to Bethlehem Center High School —one of our rivals— looking at some video footage of another player, the head coach Don Bartolomucci confided that *if he (Mr. Doba) really needed a lineman, go over to Brownsville and see me.* Back in elementary school, Mr. Bartolomucci's son and I attended Cox-Donahey together before their family moved away, across town. Through the years, it seems that Mr. Bartolomucci had, as a coach, followed me from a distance.

I was very excited; this would be my first ever

plane trip and the first time going to Indiana. Both of my parents very much like Purdue's head coach, Leon Burnette, as he had previously flown out to meet my family. And of course, *Sergeant Carter* had also offered the fair warning to him, *"you better not let anything happen to my baby."* This would be the final stage of the recruiting process, the weekend that I would visit the school and at the conclusion of it, make my decision as to whether or not I would sign on; committing to attend and play for the university. At first sight, the campus was very large, in excess of sixty thousand people. Kevin Holley, one of Purdue's football players, was the first person that I met. Having already read the press guides, I knew that he was from Washington, Pennsylvania which was only about twenty eight miles from where I lived. Though two years my senior, we instantly hit it off. I was very familiar with the high school that he had graduated from; having played against them throughout the football seasons. During the recruiting visit, I also had an opportunity to attend a basketball game which yielded some thirty-thousand people in the crowd. It was definitely an incredible experience, but at the conclusion of the weekend, I had to make a decision.

Chapter 3

◆ *Family*

ON THE LINE

John Waite's single *"I'll Be Missing You"* played through the speakers of my parent's car as we left Brownsville. My Father drove with my Mother sitting beside him, as I peered out of the window from the backseat. The three of us were set for the ten hour ride in route to the same destination that once had been just a dream and a silent prayer; said while sitting in front of the living room television. I could not wait to get *back* to Purdue, this time for the long haul. We arrived on August fifth, two days before my eighteenth birthday and checked in at the student union where I was to stay. Lorenzo Mc Cline —another player who had come from St. Louis, Missouri— and I, were the first two freshmen to report to camp. As we acclimated ourselves to the school and to the gym, I remember my Father asking me if I "was sure" that I wanted to do this, as he looked around at all of the older guys working out. Some of them were pushing twenty-two and twenty-three years of age, straddling the fence of life or even marriage, and here I am shy of eighteen— ready, willing and hungry to get down with them. My Mother, taking her own *unique* approach to manage the situation, walks over to what looks like a *nice young man* in the gym. In her most polite, yet assertive voice she asks, "Excuse me, do you go to this school?" Respectfully repositioning himself to address her, he replied, "Yes ma'am, I do." Continuing on, she points over in my direction, "well, that is my son and I want you to look after him." Agreeing to comply with her request, he walked over to me and introduced himself as Drew Banks from Killeen, Texas. It would be Drew and Kevin (Holley) that would take me under their wings and look out for me.

Reluctantly my parents left as my Mother cried. After returning to Brownsville, she called often to check in on me. The first week of camp was all freshmen. During the recruiting weekend visit, they had given me a manual —upon signing— outlining what we would be doing and what to expect. I had returned to Brownsville and studied it diligently, inside and out, sticking to the regimen. The first couple of days we had to go through some strength and conditioning exercises. I came prepared, in shape and as a result, ended up scoring very high on my speed, strength and so forth. Because of this, when we went out as a team the first day, Coach Burnette brought me up to bring everyone together and close out the practice. That was a great acknowledgement to be selected as a leader. The following week brought forth the veterans for practice. For the first few days we practiced without pads, then we all started putting them on and everything was different because now *everybody* was big, fast and strong, but I was not intimidated. Obviously, there were certain situations where some of the veteran players were there were just bigger and stronger than I, but that was more-so, just natural maturation. Football is football. I was one of the best in the country with what I was doing and they were some of the best in the country with what they were doing. We had come to meet up that is kind of how it was, and there was a level of respect amongst us. Pennsylvania is known for incredible football players and I came from the bed of football; Southwestern Pennsylvania, where they put them out. Joe Montana, Joe Namath, Dan Moreno, Charlie Unitas and Tony Dorsett all came out of the same league I came out of and they are all *'Hall of Famers.'* I came from a football pedigree. Football was everything. There was a difference, however, because I was about to embark upon college ball, where there was a whole new level of competition because everybody is there, fighting back for existence to be known, because everyone is on the same level now.

We played the inaugural game of the season against Notre Dame at the Hoosier Dome, which was also the home of the *Colts*. Going out on the field for the first time was an amazingly memorable experience. All of the excitement surrounding the warm-ups and the pre-game preparation was incredible. I was playing with some outstanding athletes like Rod Woodson, Jim Everett and Rodney

Carter, to name a few. This was the beginning of some great times; character building times and everyone was having fun. I remember getting sent into the game and how I briefly forgot everything; momentarily getting caught up in the *hoopla frenzy* of media telecasting, lights and the attention from eighty thousand cheering fans out in the stands. And it didn't stop there, nineteen eighty-four proved to be a big year for me. On top of graduating from high school and going off to Purdue University to play football, for the first time in the school's history, we went to the *Peach Bowl* in Atlanta, after beating Notre Dame, Michigan and Ohio State during the regular season.

It was also the year that my Father was indicted and went to prison for six years, eight months. He was a good man, but he got caught up trying to help the wrong people. There was still a lot of support and respect from the community because he was well known as a second generation Mason and loved as an individual. He helped a lot of people, churches and other organizations, and was even chosen of all the coal mine workers in the area, to represent and single handedly raise money for United Way, for which he raised a very large sum. It was in his nature to always fight for children, give back and sponsor programs within the community— which doesn't make it right, nor does it excuse his actions, but my point is that he was doing more with *wrong* money than a lot of people were doing with *right* money. He served federal time for drugs, to pay for his mistakes. That was a very difficult period for me; as he would only get to see me play football live one time during my college years. The rest of the times were only on television. My Father got sick while he was in prison and that is when he found out that he was diabetic.

The *Boiler Express* —the school's private jet used for our team's travel— chartered us to Atlanta, a first ever visit for me. And for making it to the *Peach Bowl*, the players were given six hundred and sixty-one dollars each for personal expense. At the time, that was a lot of money and we definitely had fun with it partying like '*rockstars*.' The game was played at the old Fulton County Stadium, but we ended up losing twenty-seven, twenty-four to the University of Virginia. I fell in love with Atlanta and knew that when I had an opportunity, would like to go back. As my freshman year concluded, I had made it on the *Dean's List* twice. The players had a study group and tutors; however it was my high school coaches that had really prepared me. I went to college focused, prepared to work, and I did everything that I was told to do. I was not a drinker nor a partier, so distractions were never a big issue. I remained grounded. For me, it was all about football.

That summer, I stayed at school working at the golf course and training. During that time, I gained nearly forty pounds and lost seven percent body fat. My body structure had more muscle and my arms had grown to twenty-three inches. It was at that point that I knew college sports truly were a business. It was made clear that the school was there to provide us an education, but we —the athletes— were there to make the school money first. It was a trade-off and no less. The coaches looked at your commitment level and staying for the summer was favored.

—People fail to realize that college athletes bring in

some ridiculously incredible revenue for the schools, which also funds the other extra-curricular activities. The sports teams are leaders in branding the school into society's popular culture. As a result, I am of the opinion that players should be paid.—

I mentally began preparing myself for the second year. By this time, I had now seen other teammates get drafted and the process, which was very intriguing to me. In addition, I had also saw teammates vanish because their grades had dropped and so forth. Understanding the two scenarios taught me the principle:

—The people you start with are not going to be the people you finish with. Stay focused, stay committed. It's all about building teams—

That is one of the biggest nuggets that I learned from college and it has nothing to do with a book. Everything that I learned in life is from being on a football field and I believe those are some of the best lessons that you can learn; how to overcome adversity, how to deal with people from all walks of life, how to come together, how to push each other and how to set goals.

—Fred Edge, an Instructor at Purdue, taught us positive imaging; playing out pictures in your mind before it actually happens. It showed me how powerful the brain is and how you can put your mind in a certain energy —or state— to obtain specific results—

Visualizing what I needed to do, I got busy. This time around, I was bigger, faster and stronger. There was positive feedback about me. One of my biggest challenges, however, was the fact that my Father was in prison. That was hard because he couldn't come to the games. I would see other parents at the games and think of my own. My Father and Mother had always come out to support me. Now, I would only speak with him every once and awhile. It was prearranged that he would call my coach's office at a designated time so we could talk. And, it was too expensive for my Mother to fly in and out from Brownsville, so my teammates became my family. Eric Forrest and I became close friends. He was from South Bend, Indiana and would take me home with him when he went. His mother became my *'surrogate mother.'* Then, I met my wife who took care of me from then on. I was very fortunate to form a lot of prodigious relationships with great friends. Many of them were Ques or Sigmas. In my junior year, I had planned to pledge for the Ques, but ended up having orthoscopic surgery on my shoulder, which prevented me from being able to do so. And I do regret, not being able to join the fraternity.

Between the fourth and fifth games of that same year, we were all sitting around, hanging out one night. My buddy Brian Jackson received a disturbing phone call from his girlfriend who was screaming and crying. She was out at a party where a guy was harassing and grabbing her. Some of my teammates and I went with Brian over to this party to check on her. Now mind you, we were going over as African-Americans in Indiana where, even in the nineteen-eighties, racism still existed. The Klan had actually been marching on our campus just a month before. So, here we are at the party where this blonde haired guy calls me a *nigger.* A fight ensues and I grab a phone off the wall and hit him with it. Eventually, we all leave.

About a week later, I go into the football complex, where there is a note on my locker instructing me to go upstairs and see the Coach. Once I arrived, he proceeded to tell me that the campus police want to see me about an incident that happened off campus. I went down and spoke with them, but was advised that I would have to go before the *Dean of Students* for a hearing. A couple of weeks prior to this altercation, our Coach had gone directly to the *President of School*s, Stephen Barry to get one of our players back in school who had been put out due to grades. Mr. Barry was a huge football fan, nonetheless, his overwriting of the Dean's ruling caused strife between the Dean and the Coach. My case is the next one up in front of the board just a couple of weeks later. During the hearing, the board puts me in a compromising situation, as they want me to reveal all of the names of the football players who were at the party the night of the incident. I refused. If I would have given them all the names of the players that were in attendance, we would not have had a football team left. Some of the people that were at the party that night are now *'NFL Hall of Famers.'* Because of my decision to take a stand, I was suspended pending their investigation which took about a week and following; I was expelled from the school. I remained in Indiana until football season was over and then I went back home to Brownsville. A number of coaches and schools called me. I could have gone to another big university, but was ready to get back playing after sitting out half of the season already. I made the decision to go to Western Kentucky University, which was probably one of the best decisions that I ever made because it really humbled me; made me appreciate playing ball more. The fact that I had a second chance, some people never get a second chance and that helped me to look back and really reflect on the decisions that I had made the night of the party. I had never grown up in that type of —racially motivated— environment for someone to call me out the way he did. My reaction was my response. In addition, the fact I was using steroids at the time, looking back, I am absolutely certain in saying it affected my emotions and the way that I reacted.

My son was born in Indianapolis just two days before I was to report to training camp for the start of my senior year. I'm playing down at *Bowling Green*, with great people around me and I'm on top of my game. Dave Roberts, the Head Coach, was probably one of the best recruiters in the country. We had a number of players that came from big schools, who had perhaps found themselves in some type of situation or dilemma. Dave made it his duty to grab the best of the best to represent for the school. And as a result of his commitment, our team had a *big school* mentality. I went from being a *big fish* to becoming a *whale*. Coaches, Scouts, Recruiters, Agents and Managers alike, are coming to practices and games to watch me play. I was starting the games and received a lot of exposure, so people would see or recognize me from television. My teammates were awesome and so were my roommates, David Smith and Brad Thomas. There was a lot of *dormradery*, we hung and had great times creating greater memories together. I took the call from Art Rooney when Rodney Carter was drafted by the Steelers; we partied, were all happy for him. Outside of school we would align together, as we were all *broke*, but we always made it work. One of us had bread, another peanut butter and somebody had jelly— it was fun. More importantly though, I was closer to home and nothing felt better than when my sister Elaine brought my Mother down, along with my brothers, for a surprise visit to see us play against the University of Louisville. It was just great to be able to have my family close again and their willingness to come out and offer their support.

Chapter 4

♦ *Family*

AFTER THE DRAFT

I went down to my apartment in Atlanta to work out. My agent had been paying for it. He had also bought me a Benz and paid for the hospital expenses when my son was born. The drafts were over and after about five months, I couldn't afford the place or the car. I had not ever prepared myself or my life for not being drafted and having a career in sports. It had been my entire life since I was six. Football was everything and being drafted as a professional player by the NFL was my plan, my ticket. I had come from a football pedigree, but for me, the drafts had come and gone. Some promises had been made, but the reality was that I had not signed any contracts and being as though I chose the football scholarship, that decision relinquished all further offers into the MLB organization. It was time for me to make some decisions because life wasn't slowing down. I know that the fight at Purdue really hurt my career. What do you do, though? It happened and I couldn't change the past. Perhaps I could have and— probably should have stayed and played at Western Kentucky for a fifth year to earn another year of eligibility; which would have helped to put the negativity of the fight situation to rest, but I was twenty-two years old, had a son and a family to take care of now; bills accumulating and people that I owed. Everyone that helped and supported me, as well as my family, up to that point— the coaches, agents and schools, they had all banked on my professional sports career, as did I. Now it seemed that I would have to head back home to

Brownsville; back to my Mother's house to try to regroup and figure out another plan.

My two sports agents continued to make calls and negotiate on my behalf as some offers came in. The Pittsburgh Steelers brought me in to work out which of course, I was excited about. In addition to it being my hometown team, a few of my best friends and college teammates were there playing, as well, so I looked forward to the prospect of joining the team and playing with them again. Head coach at the time, Chuck Noll, brought me in to the Steelers facility and told me point blank that he was going to sign me. After having me wait there about six hours, I was told they "would be in touch with me," and that they were "in negotiation with" my agent. After that, I never heard from the Pittsburgh Steelers again. I believe that my agent was probably asking for a ridiculous amount of money upfront to try and recoup for expenses of mine that they have previously covered. About nine days later, I received a call from the Houston Oilers to come in and work out followed by an offer to play in Canada for the Winnipeg Blue Bombers. As for the Oilers offer to come workout, I was so depressed and discouraged by then, that I did not go down to Texas and could not get past thinking of the cold weather or low salary up North, so I declined Canada's offer, too.

Financially things were very rough, or so I thought. To be quite frank, I had no real understanding of the true definition of rough, but would learn in the coming years. At the time, my wife and son were still living in Indiana and though she had already graduated nursing school and was working at a hospital as a R.N.; she also had my son to care for, who by now, was already a year old. My mind state after returning to Brownsville certainly was not making anything easier. I was very thankful for the support from my Wife and her Mother, and of course from my own Mother, along with the rest of my family, but I did not want to be back at home. As close as my sister Elaine and I were, she knew the devastation that I felt, and understood what I was going through so after about six months of staying at Mom's house, she invited me out to Columbus, Ohio to stay with her until I could come up with a plan. It took a couple of months before my Wife and I came to the decision that she would leave Indiana, and I Ohio; meeting at my Mother's where we would stay until we got a place together. Although with no money, there really weren't too many options, so it was into the projects that we moved —*The Snowden Terrace Housing Projects*— Fifty-Two Snowden Terrace to be exact. It would become our new residence for the next two years, before moving into another housing project. I will never forget the cost to move-in was twenty-two dollars down and twenty-two dollars for the first month's rent. Forty-four dollars is what we had to pay in order to move in, but even that was more than Tina and I had, we were *broke*. Elaine stepped in and gave us the money for the deposit and for the rent.

Snowden Terrace was not completely foreign to me. Growing up, I always knew and went to school with people that lived there and it wasn't far from my parent's home, but I could not believe that now, it was the place where my own family lived. There were many nice and kind-hearted people in the housing project that seemingly had fallen on hard times or simply did not know how to break the generational bondage of poverty. Like most, if not all of the residents there, we turned to welfare for financial assistance, as well as the W.I.C. — Women, Infants and Children— and Government Food Stamp programs to help support our family. Still apart of the 'I.T.C. —I'm Too Cool— Crew,' I wasn't working because I wanted to play ball. While the neighborhood was relatively safe, it was definitely not conducive to thriving and shattered any aspirations of hope or dreams. For me, the effect from the surroundings seemed exceedingly dismal and mentally deteriorating, like living in jail.

It was four o'clock in the morning when my Wife's water broke. For the past several months, we had prepared for the birth of our new son, having also chosen the name Derek for him. Jumping into the bucket seats of our powder blue colored *'Ford Fairmont,'* Tina and I rolled down the windows as usual, so the exhaust that would come in while driving, could escape. Just one stop first before heading to the hospital and that was to pick up my Mother. We got to her house and she carefully climbed into backseat on the passenger side and positioned herself in the middle next to my son, because the passenger floor was missing and lead straight to the ground. The deep slopes of Pennsylvania's hills never proved to be a challenge for me, as I was use to them. But this day was different because when I applied my brakes to slow down, they failed. With my Wife sitting next to me in labor, our son and my Mother in the backseat, we all began praying. I tried a couple more times and finally the brakes worked. Thank God. We made it to the hospital just in time to welcome the birth of our new healthy and beautiful baby — daughter— whom we named, Venetra.

Eventually, I got a job with Xerox working in the manufacturing end of the company. Before long though, they close the plant relocating it to New York. I grew deeply depressed and started doing drugs. My family and those around me had no idea, as I alienated myself knowing that I was not in the right frame of mind. I was below zero in life and set to head down a path of complete destruction. I didn't have any money and started bouncing checks all over town, continuing until I was arrested for it. At that point, my Father reached out to two people for them to step in and help me. One was his lifelong friend Eck Knisley, who was President of the City Council; and the other was Chief Judge Cicchetti, whose son I had grown up with. Judge Cicchetti showed favor, having knowing me and my story. He called the Magistrates that held the bad checks and told them to send all of the paperwork to him, and then he let me out of jail. That was really the turning point of my life. I had hit rock bottom. I always knew that

I had the ability to do great things, I just needed a break. Eck Knisley gave me the oxygen tank of life that I needed and brought me back up to zero. He got me involved in the community, right there in the projects where we lived. I started speaking to the residents within, getting people registered to vote, trying to clean-up the projects and encourage the children that lived there. My father and I worked together and supported Herb Mitchell's, campaign to become Magistrate. He was a local attorney, the Father of one of my childhood friends and well-liked and highly regarded man in the community. He ended up winning the race by a landslide.

Eck Knisley was acting as temporary Mayor when he called me one day and told me to come down to the Police Station. I was a little nervous, but went down anyway. Knowing my background and that I had gone to school for *Criminal Justice*, he called me into his office and asked what I thought about becoming a Constable, a position similar to that of a Sheriff. Taken back by his offer, I thought out loud, 'I was just in jail a year ago for writing bad checks. How is that going to look?' He replied simply, "Everybody needs a second chance. Everybody likes you. You come from a good family and we want to help you. I just need you to go to the courthouse and fill out some paperwork." He made it that simple. Later on in the day, I received another phone call from him and he said, "Herb Mitchell gets sworn in on Monday as Judge, and he will swear you in on Tuesday." I was very appreciative, but not everyone was happy. The Constable that had arrested me just a year before stirred up some action. He tried to do everything in his power to prevent me from being sworn in, even contacting the Governor. In his mind, he thought that I was this troubled person that would now be out in the field arresting people with him. That wasn't completely the case. Out in the field with him I would be, but troubled, I was not. I did not have a felony record; the checks were a summary offense, similar to a speeding ticket. I realized that this might be the only opportunity for a second chance and further, had I been in a big town, a second chance would have never been presented in the first place. But by being from a small community; a small town where everybody knows me, ninety-nine percent of the people were pulling for me to get back on my feet.

My position as Constable opened up additional opportunity for me two years down the line as an Account Manager with Rent-A-Center. Similar to the eviction duties as Constable, within this position I would go to holders of bad accounts and collect past due money. A gentleman named John Evans took be under his wing from a business standpoint and got me promoted to Store Manager over the Eighth and "H" Street location in Washington, D.C.; one of the roughest stores within the entire company. Utilizing my training in Law Enforcement, and because of my street savvy, I was able to turn the store around. That particular location had a high credit, which meant a significantly large percent customers were not paying. Pleased with my results of turning the store around, the company subsequently positioned me as Marketing Manager. That experience of successfully operating their business catapulted my desire to start my own.

Chapter 5

♦ *Family*

WIND BENEATH MY WINGS

My sister Elaine and I always had an insatiable relationship. Since the very beginning of my life, she has been very protective of me, always supportive of me. Even our birthdays were close, just one day apart. She always motivated me to do more, to have more, and to be more. We had an incredible relationship and even as adults, I would talk to her three or four times a week. Elaine was absolutely the strongest Black woman that I have ever met in my entire life. She was a serious Mother, a serious Wife, a serious Sister, a serious Daughter and a serious Friend. She always took care of herself and that is why I was so extremely shocked when Elaine got sick. When the

Doctor diagnosed her with cancer; giving her only six months to live, she was strong and she fought. She fought hard. Not one day did she ever say I hurt, I feel bad. In helping our Father to deal with his own illness, the Doctors would call Elaine; as she and I were the only ones that he would listen to. She and my Father had a very close relationship, even though he was not her biological, their love was undeniable. As her illness progressed, I remember looking at her lying in the bed and she said, *"I don't know how this happened to me."* I didn't know what to say, I just tried to comfort her as best I could.

My Father was a different kind of cat, a hardworking man that showed his love through providing. He might not directly say, or have those forty minute conversations with you, but his way of showing his love was through his actions. That was what he knew and I inherited the trait from him. As African-American men —sometimes— we are not good at expressing our emotions and often the best way we can express them is through something else. Obviously as I got older, my Father continued on, telling and teaching me more about life. The two of us were so close that it seemed like we were, at one time, *together* attached to my Mother's umbilical cord.

He became ill while in prison and was diagnosed with diabetes and there was nothing that I could do. In nineteen ninety-three, he began dialysis treatments. And when he told me that he needed a kidney, it did not even take me fifteen seconds to say, *'I'll give you mine.'* He looked after himself and handled his own affairs, but allowed me to move him out to Virginia to live with us for a year, and it was a blessing because the bond between my *Father*, *Wife*, *Cedric Jr.*, and *Venetra* grew. The four of them already had a close relationship, but this *time* just brought them even closer together. My Wife and Children would cook breakfast for him every morning and he would go to Cedric Jr.'s, football games; supporting and cheering him on the same way that he used to do me.

After he moved back to Brownsville we would talk every single day. Ours would be the first call of the morning and the last phone call at night. And as he grew older, my Father definitely became freer with his emotions. Every time he got ready to hang up the phone, he would say, *"Man, I love you, I'm proud of you."* He was the most providing person, always abundant; never a small figure. Either he did it *big* or he didn't do it at all. I inherited the same mindset from him and so did my children. He always pushed me and was relentless about my becoming somebody that he could be proud of. To this day, that is the one of the single-most driving forces in my life; to please my *Parents*, to please my *Dad*. My own children know that in whatever they are involved, the guiding question is, would their *Pap-Pap* be happy with what they are doing? That is the kind of influence he had in my life. And, it is why I say that I believe I had one if the best Father's in the entire world. He was insistent about my success and would always say, *"I took risks in life so that you won't have to. You get your education. You go do well. You take care of your family and don't come back to Brownsville."* After he became ill, he would tell me, *"You are not a doctor. I need a doctor,"* which meant that he did not want me to come back to Brownsville and take care of him.

Elaine and my Father had a tremendous amount of

love for my Wife, Tina. They loved, loved, loved her to death. When my Father was away in prison, the last year and a half, he was trying to get in front of the parole board and Tina would call over and over again to the point that the hearing officer asked, "who-is-this-lady." She has always supported the family. Her heart, her strength, her selflessness and her backbone has always helped keep our family together. Elaine and my Father always recognized that in Tina.

February 8, 2003, I woke up startled in the middle of the night because I dreamt that my Father passed away. Two days later on February 10, 2003, he died unexpectedly. My Aunt Deanie waited several hours before calling for ambulance. Elaine never knew that our Father passed, as she herself passed on February 14, 2003, eighteen months longer than Doctors had given her to live. She embodied the mold and the example of all that I want my own daughters to personify; and the level of integrity in which I hope that they aspire to incorporate within their own lives. She loved and protected my children as her own.

Every day, I work towards trying to create a legacy for my Father that will never be forgotten. As a third generation Mason, I just continue to do the best that I can; never wanting the *Clemons* name to ever go in vain. My Father would always say to me, *"Man, if I die today, tonight or tomorrow and you look down in the casket at me and let my Dad's name die, I will never forgive you."* As far as we know, Cedric Jr., and I are the last living *Clemons*.

Coach Tony Iacconi & Cedric

Brownsville Little League All Stars

1979

Brownsville Area High School "Falcons"

1981

Jaimie Stagesin & Cedric

Brownsville Area High School "Falcons"

1981

My Paternal Grandmother

Laura Ann McGee Clemons

My Mother

Catherine Travis Penn

My Father

Oscar "Big O" Clemons, Jr.

My Sister

Elaine Penn

Purdue University

1985

Western Kentucky University

1987

Cedric Being Sworn In As Constable for the State of Pennsylvania by Magistrate Herb Mitchell

Chapter 6

♦ *Prosperity*

SUCCESS IS A DECISION

The wireless industry was relatively new, but experiencing expediential growth because of the products. Cell phones and pagers were highly popular, however many people did not have the means to attain them. My Wife cashed in her 401K retirement fund of roughly forty-six thousand dollars and gave me to invest into *Prime Communications*, a wireless business that I started and ran from my garage with my good friend, Lonnie Robinson.

Mr. Dick Rice was the Father of my friend Rick; however, he was also very successful in the long distance arena of business. Mr. Rice took me aside one day and we had an in-depth conversation about life and business goals. Impressed with direction of our conversation, he told me that I was "too sharp" and from that point began mentoring and teaching me the correct way to set up and conduct business. Making a number of phone calls on my behalf, he set me up with a *personal accountant*, directed the bank to establish a business loan for me, and then showed me how to obtain an *authorized dealer license*. I did not realize it at the time, but twenty-three percent of the bank's assets belonged to Mr. Rice. Dick channeled me into reading, which directly helped me to learn more and expand my overall knowledge of business. Referring me to a book on *real estate and negotiation*, authored by Donald J. Trump, it was from there that I learned about *exclusivity*. It taught that if you ever want to operate retail outlets, you need to make sure that you have an *exclusivity clause* in your contract for your locations. The clause would prohibit another company from coming in and placing the type of business in that location. I included the clause in my all of my contracts. Working hard day and night, the business took flight; eventually developing into a chain of stores throughout a handful of states. And while the chains were successful, in the early days, I did, from time-to-time, have to use my wife's paycheck to cover payroll. It was that ten dollar —Donald J. Trump— book that help to change my life, giving me the ability to create leverage within my business. A few years later, a major wireless company wanted to expand.

I was driving down a Jacksonville, Florida highway in my blue *Corvette* when my Wife called and said that the executives from —a major wireless company— had just contacted the office looking for me. "What is it about, what did you do?" she immediately asked. In turn I told her that 'I have no idea, I haven't done anything.' My phone number was forwarded to the company and I received a phone call shortly thereafter requesting for me to fly out to New York the following day to meet with the company; and that they had already purchased my first-class ticket. That night I stayed up racking my brain, trying to figure out what they could possibly want. As scheduled, I took the flight and headed over to their office. Just as I stepped inside, the Receptionist greeted. "You must be Cedric Penn." I responded, 'yeah, though I don't know if that is a good thing or a bad thing.' Escorting me over to the conference room, she advised that the executives were waiting on me. As the meeting convened, one of the executives inquired as to whether I wanted the good news or the bad new first. Opting for the bad, he continued, "Do you remember when we toured your store?" I honestly did not. It seems that the company had toured my stored a year or two prior to this meeting. He then asked, "Do you remember how much you said you would sell your business for?" Again, I did not recall. Placing a manila folder on the conference table before me, he finally said, "well, we cannot give you what you are asking for, but we can give you this. The catch is that there is no thinking about it. It's either right now or nothing." Inside of the folder lay a check for one million dollars. He told me that the company would do their due-diligence and if everything checked out, they would disburse the rest of the money. I signed the agreement and quickly walked out of the office, immediately calling my Wife. "They gave you a million dollars?!" she exclaimed. As part of the deal, I would also sign on as Director of Marketing for the company.

Twenty-seven months prior, I was in a financial squeeze and needed ten thousand dollars to cover payroll because I had opened stores a bit too quickly. I called one of my brothers and offered him forty-nine percent of the company, in exchange. He would not budge. Instead, it was my Mother-in-Law whom gave me the money and after I sold the business, she would not even allow me to pay her back. Never in our most vivid imagination, did we foresee a forty-six thousand dollars retirement fund, ten dollar book and additional ten-thousand dollar investment combined with diligence, sacrifice and hard work to return a six million dollar profit.

The new position offered an arena of business

development affixed on an entirely different scale. I welcomed the personal growth that came along with it. My Wife and I purchased land and begun building our dream home. As I was heavily focused on the wireless industry, so were the majority of our monetary investments. In addition, I had a network marketing business that I was actively building. I spent the next two years out in the field for the company. In one of those two calendar years, I remember being on the road working two hundred and twenty-one days. I began to feel as though financially my family was secure and that I was in a position of which I could now retire. And that is exactly what I did, I resigned from my job. A move that I would —not long after— realize I had made too soon. The tragedy of nine-eleven occurred and I lost in excess of one million dollars cash in the subsequent stock market decline. I had my *Network Marketing* business, but it was not anywhere close to what I needed to cover our expenses and sustain my family. Very quickly the empire around us began to crumble. I tried to utilize every resource available to stabilize our finances, but no matter what I tried, it just was not enough.

—*It is to be said that one does not inherit success by simply waking up one day, nor that an empire has been built on a solid foundation because you were able to elevate to the top floor. The road to success is a constant and lifelong journey, and contrary to grave misunderstanding, the hardest part is not becoming successful, rather it is staying successful*—

Through business ventures we had found success and garnered a substantial amount of income, turning our life around entirely. Now however, time was rapidly elapsing. From the outside looking in, it appeared that I was on top of my game. My family, personal appearance, truck and home— all seemed to be intact. The truth of the matter was something completely different.

It was a regular Saturday afternoon when I pulled into the gas station to pump my last twenty dollars. While doing so, a gentleman approached me and simply asked, "Do you keep your options open about making money from home?" 'They are way open,' I said without hesitation, yet refraining from further detail. He handed me a CD with his name and phone number marked on the outside and that was it. I jumped back into my truck, popped the CD in, got on the freeway and drove one exit before pulling over at the rest stop and dialing Ron Harrelson, the man who handed me the CD just five minutes before. When he answered, all I said was 'I need to go ahead and do this.' Completely caught off guard, he did not say much before I added, 'if you want to sign me up, you will be at my house tomorrow.' There was an ice storm the next day and where we lived; there were neither trucks nor salt for the roads. Nonetheless, Ron made the four hour drive down to my house. At first glance, he was able to tell by outward appearance that we must have had some sort of success in business, or at the least respectable careers, which hopefully reassured him that he had not made the trip in vain. Ron came inside and signed me into the company. Afterward he told me how he had just left a big Super Saturday Event at the time in which we met, and that I was his first exposure thereafter. He left my home and I immediately went to work. Grabbing a notebook and a pen, I made my way into the living room and sat down in my big brown *lazy boy* chair, proceeding to commence writing my contact list. But, before I could even begin, the tears began streaming down my face as I started praying and crying, *'God please help me to get my family out of this situation.'* Honestly I believe that was the first time in my life that I was *truly* humble and willing to listen to the direction of others. Continuing on that Sunday, as well, the coming week, I got busy on the phone calling everybody I knew, anyone that I could think of; in essence, dialing for dollars. I was in a bad state financially as things were spiraling downwards. After losing close to ninety percent of our cash investments in the demise of the stock markets, our house went into foreclosure, our credit cards were maxed out and my truck payments were behind and it was on the heels of being repossessed. The next weekend I went out to the scheduled fast start training meeting. This time I wanted to have all the knowledge I could about building the business. However, as quickly as I tried to bandage the wounds in our life, more that would appear. The week following the training, my truck was repossessed and two weeks after that, I was driving down the highway in my wife's car while on the phone with a prospect. Dropping the phone on the floor, I reached down to pick it up. Not realizing, I ran the red light and as another car entered the intersection and t-boned me. Needless-to-say, because of our financial situation, the insurance had lapsed and my Wife's car was now demolished. In addition, a judgment will soon be entered against me for the damage to the other vehicle. In desperate need of a car, I go down to the rental company with no money and no credit cards. It just so happens that the rental associate is a fraternity brother, a Mason. He gives me the car instructing me that I had "better have the money to pay for it" when I return. Everything that could go wrong was going wrong when I got started. That is why when I hear people say, "It's hard. I don't have anyone to talk to," I cannot accept it. I had to get busy. I used the same mentality that I saw people using out on the streets and I put it into business. They were out there pushing something that is bad for your body, and I got out there and started pushing something that was good for the body. I did whatever I had to do; slept in my car and washed up in the bathrooms at the gas stations. I kept three dress shirts hanging in the back of my car and a trunk full of ties. If I happened to spot the same person two days in a row, I would run to the car and switch ties. And since the truck had been repossessed and I totaled my Wife's car, I was rolling around in a *hooptie*, so if I found myself talking to a prospect in a parking lot, I would just make my way over to the nicest car out there and hope that the owner didn't come before I finished my presentation. The company paid daily and had direct deposit so, no matter where I was, I would just call my Wife and make sure the deposit posted so that she would have money for the bills and children. Change did not happen instantly, but slowly things did begin to turn around.

Chapter 7

♦ *Prosperity*

IT'S BETTER TO WATCH A LEADER THEN LISTEN TO ONE

Over the next two years, my business grew, but building was not easy to do and there were times when I became frustrated, discouraged and ready to throw in the towel. One month I made twenty-six thousand dollars and the next month I made six dollars, due to charge-backs. Dave Savula taught me, "It's is better to watch a leader then listen to one."

I can recall picking up the phone one day and calling Dale Calvert's office. Though I did not know him personally, I had been purchasing his books and tapes, "The Secrets of A Millionaire in Network

Marketing," and I hoped that he could help to guide me in the direction that I needed to go. A lady answered the telephone and I asked to speak with Mr. Calvert. A few seconds later, a gentleman came on the line and asked how he could help me. Introducing myself, I told him that I buy his books and tapes would love the opportunity to sit down and speak with him sometime. He gave me an address, told me that he was there every day from nine a.m. to five p.m., and then hung up the phone. I walked into the next room where my Wife was standing and asked her how much money we had. She answered, "Not much, but I know what you are about to do." Heading towards the bedroom, she got the bank card and walked back out, handing it to me for gas. I got into the car and made the five hour trip. When I arrived at the office, the lady who answered the phone earlier, Dale's wife, greeted me. She called to the back for him and as he walked out, the first thing that caught my attention was his luminous wrist watch. We spent the afternoon discussing the struggles that I was having and Dale got me on track and he was the start of my making big money in network marketing. Before I had just willed my way to a couple hundred thousand, but this time I was duplicating my way. Without Dale Calvert, I would not be where I am today. He saved my career and when I got ready to leave, he had his wife pull a set of his books and audio and video training sets. As she began to do so, I told him that I could not afford to pay for them. Dale said, "Don't worry, reach down into your organization and pay it forward."

"Raising A Giant" and "Feeding A Giant" were two books by Bob Crisp, that I had purchased. At the time, I was living in California and he was, as well.

I reached out to him; giving him a phone call, and he just so happened to answer. We scheduled to meet for coffee. In the forty five minutes to an hour that we spent, Bob showed me from a whole new perspective, how to build a big business in *Network Marketing*. Meeting with Bob Crisp took me to a multi-million dollar mentality.

There was a man that I received mentorship from, he is one of the best in the world. Respecting his privacy, I will simply refer to him as *Chase*. At the time, he was making one quarter of one million dollars per week in *Network Marketing*. We met through a mutual friend when I attended a leadership convention in Utah, and afterwards was invited by the mutual friend to hang out with him, along with some of his other friends, who came and picked us up from the hotel. It began to snow a little bit and *Chase* said that he wanted to stop off and check on his ATV's, as a couple of them were in the shop and he wanted us to be able to ride. We made it to the shop, however, while were all standing inside talking, a truck pulled up outside. *Chase* asked the salesman "Is that new inventory? Can I go take a look at it?" The salesman said, "Yeah, go ahead." As he began to walk out, I follow behind— as I have always been infatuated with bikes. We looked at them and then proceeded to walk back inside the store as he jokingly asked, "Can you get on one of those, Cedric?" 'Absolutely,' I quickly responded. Then he told the salesman, "I want to buy an ATV." The salesman asked, "The ones in here?" And *Chase* said, "No, the ones outside." Indirectly refusing, the salesman then said, "The ones outside are not prepped and ready to go. We don't even have the inventory list for them yet, there is no way we can sell them." *Chase*, not accepting the salesman's position replied, "Well I need them prepped and ready because I have friends coming up to my house and I want them to have a good time." Just doing as he was trained, the salesman held his ground, "There is no way that we can sell you those. They are not ready." But *Chase* had a few tactics of his own and was *not* going to be outdone by anyone at that point, *especially* not the salesman. Calmly he said, "I want to buy them." "Who is your Manager, can you go get him?" Finally, the salesman went to the back of the shop and told the Manager that he was wanted up front. Now the Manager comes out, "How can I help you?" Assertively, Chase replied, "I want to buy the trailer." Puzzled, the Manager questioned "The trailer?" He said, "Yeah, I want to buy the trailer and all of the ATV's on it." There were about eight ATV's total. The Manager still did not understand what was transpiring. He is probably thought this was some kind of prank or something as he dismissingly responded, "We can't sell them, we don't know what the cost is and we don't have the paperwork." *Chase* said, "That's okay. I'll just leave you a blank check and when you guys figure everything out, let me know and I will adjust my balance." The Manager just stood there with a blank look on his face like, *what are you talking about?* Now the original salesman steps in to intercede. Taking the Manager to the back, he explains who *Chase* is. Suddenly, the Manager walked back up to the front and simply says, "Okay." Except, there was one last instruction for the Manager. *Chase* further stipulated, "Everything has to be at my house within the next hour or two and I mean the trailer, too. I want to buy the trailer that's pulling them too, so that I can pull them whenever I need to." "Ohhh-kay," concluded the Manager.

―*I gained a lot from that experience. Society likes to label and associate us, especially African-Americans, as D.E.A. ―Drugs, Entertainment, Athlete―, if we make a substantial amount of money. And that is not the case. Chase is not African-American, but my point is that we have to stop allowing society to dictate our direction and our potential. But first and foremost, we as individuals have to stop placing limitations on our own success. The next man, or woman, is not necessarily stronger than you; he or she just got into the right opportunity and went to work. Spending the time with Chase really opened my eyes as to how big this industry really is, what kind of leverage people really have, and what kind of wealth is really generated within the Network Marketing Industry.―*

Ken was another man that I received Mentorship

from. One day the two of us discussed the negative connotation associated with the *Network Marketing Industry* and how people think that it is a *scam* or a *scheme* when it really is not. There are people who scam or scheme, but the industry itself, is not a scam or a scheme. Ken shared with me how his brother had been the most negative person around him when it came to his working in this industry. And how he had struggled in twenty-eight companies before finally achieving success in the company that the two of us were now a part of. Ken told me how, in the past, he would attend family functions where his family members would talk about his failures. His brother would say I want to take a picture of you, so when you have children and grand-children, I can show them how big of a failure their *grand-pop* was because he kept getting *scammed* and *schemed* in Network Marketing. So one Christmas holiday, his brother was visiting and Ken said, "I have to go run some errands and do some banking. Would you like to come along?" When he got to the bank, he and his brother stood at the teller's window, as he stuck his check through. The bank teller asked, "What would you like to do with this?" and Ken responded, "I want to cash my check." The teller asked him to please wait a minute, as she needed to go get her Manager. She did and the Manager approached the teller's window and asked, "Mr. Redlands, you want all two hundred and thirty-one thousand?" Ken answered, "Yeah, I want it all in cash," then he looked over at his brother and asked, "Did you get that on tape? That was two hundred and thirty-one thousand dollars that I made working from home."

—That story showed me the big picture of the industry and the outcome you can have if you get around the right people and truly humble yourself; doing the right things, but more importantly, not letting anyone derail your focus.—

I spoke at a *Breakout Session* in Norfolk, Virginia which afforded me the opportunity to converse with two of the most *profound* people in business today, as well as in history; Donald J. Trump and General H. Norman Schwarzkopf, Jr. I happened to run into Donald Trump, literally, as I was walking out of the *green room*. We stopped for a few minutes, having a brief conversation. Trying to interview him, he had more questions for me. He did, however, leave me with a couple of key points that I have kept and utilized ever since. The first being, "The difference between a wealthy person and a broke person is the ability to stay focused." And the second that wealthy people, "Work on their strengths and manage their weaknesses." He also gave me assurance that I was on the right track.

General H. Norman Schwarzkopf, Jr. was probably the most confidant person that I have ever met. Given the opportunity, I wanted to ask him about the war because I was intrigued by it. I asked him how he prepared for the *Gulf War* and with confidence he replied, "I had been waiting my whole life for that phone call. I knew we were going to attack and I knew what I was going to do. I was excited about the opportunity; to show them what I had learned over the years."

—That was a life and business changing conversation. Coming from the perspective of a man who has reached the highest rank in the military, his ability to connect with the troops was apparent. I had a renewed outlook on *America* and what we stand for; as well, a complete understanding as to the level of commitment from the troops in the military. General Schwarzkopf, Jr. was so strong, exceptionally confidant and absolutely motivational. I would have gone out and put a military uniform on for him.—

Chapter 8 ♦ Prosperity

THE POWER OF CULTURE

Most do not realize, but *Network Marketing* is an industry like no other. Similar to Sports and Entertainment; it can generate long-term, steady and residual income, yet merge the significant principles of the Finance and Investment Industries. There is a substantial amount of money involved, so the stakes are tremendously high. As a result, *competition*, *greed*, *power struggles* and *set-ups*, are far greater than the traditional *corporate business world* and its politics. *Network Marketing* is not an arena built for everyone, but do not be discouraged as there are greater advantages for the one willing to step out of his comfort zone and train to enhance his personal and business development. It is an incredible industry and one that offers a level playing field for individuals from all walks of life and all educational backgrounds to attain the lifestyle that they desire; to build a business around your life, instead of vice-versa and from the comfort of your home office. It gives people an opportunity to have major success without having major assets to create success. And this industry creates more millionaires than any other.

Unfortunately, many people that got involved in *Network Marketing* very early on did not fully understand it, and as a result, a lot of people oversold the industry by telling others that they would get rich— quick. A lot of people got burned because they got involved for the wrong reasons. True to form, this is a very powerful industry and you can get rich, but you have got to *'go to work.'* The stigma that has been placed on the *Network Marketing* industry is unfounded. Of sixty-six hundred operating *network marketing* companies; only a few, a small percentage —perhaps half or maybe even one percent— are bad. Even in that, it is no different than traditional companies of *Corporate America*, and even globally. But anytime you have people, you'll have risk. The greatest tool that I think people miss in this industry is the personal growth and development. They focus on the income and do not take into consideration the skills derived from personal growth and development; the training, mentorship and all that you learn in *Network Marketing* is related to personal growth. And it is priceless. We save lives and marriages and help to change people because of the training and support and also because of the relationships that we build.

Dave Johnson was the first person to expose me to Network Marketing back in nineteen eighty-eight. Ironically, I played football at Purdue with the son of Richard De Vos, founder of the same company Dave shared with me. Imagine if I had joined four years earlier while in college, the business empire that I could have built and the subsequent revenue that I could have generated as a result. Never-the-less, I joined the company under Dave, but did not do anything within because my life at the time was in such turmoil. A year later, my Wife was presented, through her co-worker, with another network marketing business opportunity —which to date is— still a major force within the industry. She joined, but due to the fact that our day-to-day life was one year deeper engrossed by environmental despair and financial devastation, we could not see beyond the confines of our existence.

I reached out to cross-line leadership for guidance. It was Dave Savula —whom I hold in the highest regard, along with his wife— that really taught me about working on myself. Life is about confidence and courage. You have to work on yourself before you can work on any business. I cross-lined because the person who had recruited me, had not recruited anyone else, so he really did not know what to do and neither did the up-line in our group. Because of all of the mentorship that I received, I started investing fourteen to sixteen hours per day into the business, beginning each, with a two to three hour course of personal development; praying, meditating and listening to tapes— working on myself. Personal development is one of the core principles of success. You can teach the right person the right skills, but if they are not in the right frame of mind, they cannot absorb the information. My mindset became I have done it before and I can do it again. It took about six months, but things began to start turning around.

I remember like it was yesterday, the day that I made the decision to be successful in Network Marketing. There was a big conference being held in Philadelphia, Pennsylvania. I, being the self-proclaimed leader of our group orchestrated the trip for us to attend. There were a number of us going so I rented a van and reserved the hotel room. Not having too much money, I fluctuated between about five hundred dollars cash and a credit card. We were leaving from Charleston, South Carolina —approximately five hundred and sixty miles away— and had to stop in Baltimore, Maryland to pick up a friend and one of our team members, Tracy Hayes from the *Baltimore Airport*. Upon arriving, we took my Wife's clothes out of the back and placed them on top of the van to put his luggage in. However, it was not until we reached Philly, that we remembered Tina's clothes, which at that point had blown away somewhere along the drive. It was also at that point that we realized *why* the strange man had been pointing to us and trying to get our attention while we drove. My Wife was *pissed-off*. Once we made it to the hotel, I let everyone out and went to park the van. As I got out, there was a white envelope lying on the ground. Not sure whether or not I was being set-up, I looked around before opening it to find three one hundred dollar bills enclosed. With money in hand, I proceeded into the hotel lobby to check-in. It is funny now, though it wasn't then, I remember the reservationist asking how many keys I needed; thinking to myself, 'we need eight,' I replied two. Various company conferences took place within our organization over the next two days. But it was the leadership event that weekend recognizing the

Black Tie Ring Earners that had the greatest impact on me. Towards the end of the evening function; just before the Grand speech was made by the CEO, two ushers began escorting a gentleman across the stage to the microphone. The crowd in the room began to laugh, as we all thought that it was a skit being performed. As he began speaking, the crowd settled in attention and it quickly became clear that this was in fact, not a scripted entertainment performance; but a successful business owner of one of the biggest syndicated radio stations in the world. I watched him and listened attentively realizing that success is absolutely a decision; it is your choice to do or not to do. There is no excuse for success; likewise, there is no excuse not to be successful. That fact that he stood on the stage, unable to see us sitting in front of him was irrelevant. The lesson of the night was that all of us were sitting in the light making excuses while he stood in the dark and creating a legacy. From that night forward, I tried to stop consciously making excuses; rather seeking mentorship from the most successful leaders in the business industry. Darnell Self and Rodney Summerville really reinforced the power of culture. Their teachings, along with their teams, have always been something that I look up to. Dave Savula, Eric Worre and Jerry "Rhino" Clark became influential *mentors*; always there for me helping me to complete my skills; always keeping it real with me; telling me what I need to hear and not just what I want to hear. Those are great mentors, and great friends.

I received a phone call from a mutual friend about the start-up of a new company. Actually the company wasn't new, it was about five years old, but the original CEO had died from a heart attack.

The new owner was Karl Braselton, a very well-respected man that I knew from the industry. I felt it was something that I needed to go take a look at so I flew out to meet him, as well as the executive team. We put together some ideas along with some resources, and then I went to work. After returning home, I put together a team and flew some of my key people out to Salt Lake City, Utah to test the products. We tasted the products and liked them going forward, executing our due diligence. At time, the company was paying in unilevel comp plans which meant that I would have access to the volume and income, irrespective of the level, width or depth, which was a great thing. My team and I began building that company. We were able to attract some great people about two and a half years into it —on the back end, no less— generating a substantial amount of income. At that time, there were three master distributor lines and my organization, The Diamond Network, began dominating the company; contributing to eighty-five percent of the company revenue from a producer stand point. My downline expanded in excess of forty thousand people, as I became the *Top Income Earner* within the company three years straight.

There are not many *big* African-American leaders within the industry. To me, that in itself is an entirely different level of *responsibility*, therefore it is important to ensure that I play my position as a good role model...

Chapter 9

♦ *Finalé Revealed*

From Broke, Busted & Disgusted To ~Faith, Family & Prosperity~

As I lay face down on the pavement, I could hear five or six cars pass me by. I began to recite Psalm 23:

"The LORD is my shepherd; I shall not want.

He maketh me to lie down in green pastures: he leadeth me beside the still waters.

He restoreth my soul: he leadeth me in the paths of righteousness for his name's sake.

Yea, though I walk through the valley of the shadow of death, I will fear no evil: for thou art with me; thy rod and thy staff they comfort me.

Thou preparest a table before me in the presence of mine enemies: thou anointest my head with oil; my cup runneth over.

Surely goodness and mercy shall follow me all the days of my life: and I will dwell in the house of the LORD for ever."

I got through the passages once, and then began again. The second time towards the end, I stopped and— I could not feel my legs. It was at that point I pleaded: God, if you are going to take me, please take me in front of my family; don't let me die on the side of the road. I heard a voice say, "I'm not going to let you die" and it kind of startled me. I thought someone was standing behind me talking, so I tried to roll over but, there wasn't anyone. The cars were going by fast and— I knew that the voice I heard was *God*. Before He spoke to me, I was in pain. Afterwards, I was no longer.

—I lay helpless, unable to move and at the mercy of only God, as His grace would be the only way my life would be spared—

And I undoubtedly knew the reason for the accident. Events began to replay like slow-motion scenes from a movie: my family — childhood — church — little league — the truck accident — college — the NFL — the projects — drugs — politics — business deals— money — death — cars — women — extortion — and again — my family. Except, it wasn't at all a movie that I had ever chosen to stop and watch, not even at this very moment in which I lay on the ground; as I was not here of my own will. I remained conscious the entire time. Looking back, I'm sure it was so—that at a later point, I would be able to document this testimony. I knew that just a few moments earlier I had been in Gwinnett County; right outside of Atlanta, Georgia riding my Harley Davidson down Lawrenceville Highway at Ronald Regan Parkway. I was enjoying the ride while listening to my favorite R & B group, *The Isley Brothers*. It was Tuesday, December 16th, 2008; just nine days before Christmas. As I proceeded through the intersection, a black truck disregards the light as it came through striking me, and throwing my body into the air. I had not been driving my Harley down the road recklessly or not paying attention; that was not the case. The woman traveled with her baby in the back seat, and on the same side as the impact, no less. She never got out to see if I was alive. However, the real reason for this accident was because I had been operating my personal vehicle; my life, in a reckless manner and I had lost focus and stopped paying attention to what was taking place around me. To whom much is given, much is required. And no matter what high level of status or notoriety has been willed into one's life, God's will— always— prevails. And the absolute truth was that I had forgotten where from, my blessings came. God was in control, He always had been. But it was my thinking that I could be everything to everybody, flip my priorities upside-down, placing prosperity before family and faith instead of in its correct order; Faith, Family & Prosperity and everything would be 'all good' because I was still helping others and giving back. But, it wasn't all good because I had allowed my life to become all about money, power and women. All of the success; the tapes, the videos, the money, the speaking engagements, the Bentley, the jewelry, the trips around the world, the cars, having all the women I wanted— now overshadow what my true beliefs were and are; what life is really about. Every day, I got further and further away from my principles. I stayed on the road constantly, not stopping to take time for my family. Then I let my faith start slipping. Instead of going to church on Sundays, I would go to functions. And, though I've never been much of a drinker, I always enjoyed being in the presence of where the action was— the parties and so forth but, with that of course, comes the women. I hung out with some of the biggest stars in the world because we were in the same circle of people. They were big in their own right and I was big in my own right. We had our entourages and the paparazzi would hang out with us. I earned a lot, but I gave a lot too and I helped a lot of people along the way from an intellectual, as well as, a financial stand point.

Now, here I am on the side of the road, alone and critically injured. God was making His will clear to me and making sure I knew it and that I would never again forget the truth. Simply taking away the money was not going to get through to me. He had allowed me to make millions before- multiple times, and to also lose millions- multiple times. Yet and still, continuing to show favor each time I rebuilt. The problem, however, was that I had ignored the teachings and as a result, not learned from the lessons. One of the key components of a great leader is his able ability to stay focused.

— Study to show thyself approved unto God, a workman that needeth not to be ashamed, rightly dividing the word of truth— II Timothy 2:15

A moment or so later, an unexpected touch to my neck caused me to jump; which in turn, startled what would be a man checking for my pulse. I don't believe he thought that I was alive. He asked my name and if I knew where I was. Due to the severity of my injuries I could not see him but responded, 'Cedric Penn, I was on my bike.' The male voice then inquired as to whether I had a phone on me. I told him to look in my right pocket. I could feel him move my body to get to the phone. I said, just press number one; my number one is my Mom. Following just as I instructed, the male voice on my end asked, "Is this Cedric Penn's mother?" I could hear my mother's voice coming through the speaker of the phone as she responded, "Who is this? Yes, that's my baby!" At forty-one years old, I was still her baby. I told the still unidentified man to put the phone down by my mouth. As I called out her name she asked, "Wayne, is that you?" Of my family and childhood friends; most all called me Wayne —short for my middle name 'Dewayne'— Responding, I said, yeah Mom, I was in a bad motorcycle accident. Immediately panicking, she frantically cried out to the house for help, "Your brother is hurt, your brother is hurt" and yelling, "Is my baby dead?" The male voice responded with urgency, "No, he is not dead, but he *is* seriously injured." I remember the last thing I said was, 'Mom just get down here; I'm hurt real bad, just get down here.' Assuring me as my Mother always would, she replied "Baby, I'll get there as quickly as I can," as the faint sound of blaring sirens began coming from a distance. Back at home, my wife and I had a disagreement, an argument. I left out on the ride without saying anything to her— or my children, not even goodbye. Now here I am lying on the ground not knowing if I will ever again have the opportunity to see their faces, or if it *is* that time, say goodbye and tell them I love you.

Paramedics delivered me to the Gwinnett County Medical Center Trauma Unit at two forty-seven p.m. I was in critical condition, yet still conscious as the team of doctors ran my body through the MRI machine, twice. I remember hearing the female voices call out all of the injuries to my body and everything that was going to have to be repaired, "crushed pelvis, twenty-three fractures in right arm, crushed right elbow, broken left wrist, broken right wrist, crushed nasal, numerous facial fractures, jawbone bone loss, eight teeth knocked out...." as the voices continued calling out my other fractures and injuries, all I knew was that I was in excruciating pain from my arm as I lay on the hospital gurney. Then I heard the familiar voice of my son, Cedric Jr., call out for me— from somewhere in that emergency room. It was followed by high pitched yells from my daughter, Venetra and my wife, Tina. I was so thankful to be able to hear and speak to them one more time. God was doing just as He had promised out on Lawrenceville Highway. He was not going to let me die. As they rushed me into what would be eighteen hours of surgery, I told my daughter, 'you will always be daddy's little girl.'

It was Mother that called my Tina and informed her of my accident. But, the man whom first called my Mother; the one who touched my neck, asked my name, moved my body as he reached into my right pocket for my phone…. He— vanished into thin air. Not the Police, Lawyers, Investigators,

Paramedics; Eyewitnesses nor anyone else have ever been able to identify him— let alone, locate him. But I know he was there. And my Mother spoke to him.

Following surgery, I remained in a coma for two more days. My true loved ones stepped up and showed their brilliant colors with genuine thoughts and prayers, well-wishings, calls, cards, visits and offerings of "whatever I can do." All of my family was by my side at the hospital, as well as at home, around the clock- even through the coming months of recovery. Countless Friends and Business Partners also sat by my side supporting and helping me any way they could; as I was unable to do for myself. Bruce Taylor, Brent "Batman" Jones, George "Icky" Green, Derek "D.K." Green sat by my side every day. If I needed or wanted anything, no matter the hour —day or night— they were there for me.

—It is ultimately in your hour of need that you learn who and where your true support comes from; who is covering your back to protect you and who is covering your back, just waiting for the perfect opportunity to stab you. I believe that everything happens in life the way it is meant. The harder and more challenging events are caused for you to reassess your life; to help put it all in perspective—

The haters showed up too, and in full force. Literally at the exact hour that I was fighting for my life, board meetings were strategically being scheduled in different parts of the country, with the sole agenda to disintegrate my position within and oust me out of the company that I was a part of; the company that I, along with its President, Braden Seward, help to build— Zielar International. Unbeknownst to the independent distributor base of the company, problems separate from the controversial compensation plan change had begun to ensue behind closed doors. Sometime within the last six months prior to (this accident), I started becoming distracted and wasn't paying a lot of attention to leadership. I guess that I was at a point where I could appreciate and enjoy life again after going through so many roller coasters in life and business. Financially, I was back on top, making a whole lot of money, buying whatever I desired, even having my own personal car collection including a couple of Mercedes, Range Rover, Escalade, Jaguar, Lexus, Chargers and two

Harley-Davidsons. But the whole downfall— let me repeat, the whole downfall was when I bought my Bentley. The *Big Boys* did not like that. Greed set in as Zielar executives began going around publically stating that I was making too much money. Corporate political tension and competition surmounted as did the financial pressures, causing unrest amongst the already unsound executive board members under the leadership of Mr. Braselton— whom was on leave from the company, out on a mission. Zielar President, Braden Seward contacts me and begins telling me of his financial distress due to the expenses associated with the medical care of his parents out in Las Vegas. He then threatened that if I did not give him money, that he will terminate me from the company. Mind you, this is the same man that I worked with building Zielar. Over a very short period of time, Braden Seward extorted what would amount to nearly two-hundred thousand dollars in cash from me, in addition to making me purchase him a Harley-Davidson motorcycle.

Upon returning from his last mission, still prior to this motorcycle accident, Mr. Braselton, immediately wanted to change the compensation plan from a unilevel to a binary, which would instantly cut my income some tens of thousands of dollars per month. There is no doubt in my mind that this restructure plan was strategically being placed as a direct result of the income being generated by myself and my organization, The Diamond Network, as it was the largest — of three — master distributor lines in the company, and accounted for approximately eight-five percent of the company's distributor based revenue from a producer standpoint. On top of that, they decide to take my two biggest legs and put under Daren

Easley (Mr. Braselton's brother-in-law) and Doug Monroe, causing instant controversy, as well as strife within my organization because we were the founding distributors in the company and now everybody's check in our organization was being cut. As my team's checks went down, the other master distributor teams' checks went up. I immediately spoke with Mr. Braselton, lobbying and fighting for my team; for what was right and I created an environment where Mr. Braselton agreed to subsidize the income of the people whose checks went down until their checks went back up. He did however, two months later; two months into the agreement on December 16th, 2008, I am involved in this life-changing motorcycle accident. The following day, the corporate executives of Zielar International scheduled meetings, held conference calls and the agreement that Mr. Braselton and I had come to, immediately ceased.

Neither the company, nor any of its representatives made calls, visits or implied any concern with regards to my well-being. The only question they asked my Wife was, "When is he coming back?" And, little did I know, the events leading up to and just after this accident were only prelude of that which was yet to come over the next eighteen months. Members of my own organization, The Diamond Network, people that my family and I had regarded as friends and helped over the years; even the women, with whom I placed my trust and formed a close and intimate relationship with would all soon turn on me in exchange for a payoff check from Zielar.

She was a woman whom I had been involved with for many years. We met about ten years earlier when my wife and I were separated, back when my wireless business was booming. And at the time, I had no inclination of reconnecting with my wife. After I sold the wireless business and later after my stocks went under, as a result of nine-eleven, and my losing a million dollars and other investments respectively, she was there and when I was in a bind or didn't have what I needed, she helped me. Once business bounced back for me, I took care of her; bought her a car, jewelry, lavish lifestyle, etcetera. Later, however, my Wife and I did reconcile, though I continued to take care of this other woman because through the good and the bad she had been there, so I felt like I was indebted to staying with and helping her because she done the same for me. Down the line though, the situation caused some controversy. She came to the hospital to visit, never wanting to see anything bad happen to me— that is, until I stopped taking care of her in the coming months, at which point she began circulating lies and trying to create a lot of drama; ultimately collaborating with Zielar and others, as they put their heads together and created turmoil. An African-American man with power and money in Network Marketing; having access to everything you need in the company. Be careful, that is when problems will start to arise. You have got to stay grounded. **F**ollow **O**ne **C**ourse **U**ntil **S**uccessful. I lost focus. But, I also believe that it is the reason why I am still here; because I sowed a lot of good seeds and I gave back.

I forgive anybody. I don't forget, but I forgive. I know that everybody does certain and sometimes out of character decisions when they are under pressure. In my opinion, Keith Braselton is a good person, a noble person even, and if he knew some of the things that take place when he is not around, they would not continue. The problem is, however, when you own a company, you own their issues. That is just part of being an owner. You cannot take the good and leave the bad. The fact of the matter is that, Mr. Braselton has some bad executives working around him and unfortunately it is going to cost him millions of dollars. And that is a shame because Zielar has great products, but the leadership is not there. We all make mistakes and consequently have to be accountable.

As I lay on the ground I remember thinking, *if I die today, there was nothing else money could have ever bought me; nothing else I can say I want to do*. From a material standpoint, I have had everything that I have ever wanted. At the same time, if I had died that day in the motorcycle accident, there are some promises that I would have left unfulfilled, some thoughts that would have gone unshared, some lessons that would have went untaught and some misconceptions that would overshadowed my purpose in life and my desired legacy. I would have wished that people had gotten a chance, or perhaps just taken the time to get to know the real me, Cedric Dewayne Penn Clemons: Son, Father and Friend; seeing the personal side of me, one that very few people know. Most times, people only see or acknowledge me from a business standpoint; reducing who I am to that of Cedric Penn, the Network Marketing Professional *persona* that they see, know or have heard of. If I could do it all over again, but I cannot edit my life, it's not possible for any one of us — I have no regret — and I did not die December 16th, 2008; physically, spiritually, emotionally or mentally. The reel of life continues and as it only rolls forward, I live each new day to the maximum. This time around, I am allowing myself to be more transparent and more personable. I am letting people get closer to me, to know who I am and where I come from. Before, I couldn't do that; you really can't be transparent when you have multiple households. But now that the weight of the world has been lifted off of me from a relationship standpoint, I don't have that struggle anymore. I know who I am and where I am at in life. I am defined. You cannot be everything to everybody. I use to try— try to please everybody, but you can't; it is not possible. You've got to stay in your lane and make the people happy that are close to you; loving them with all that you have.

I believe the biggest misconception people have about me from a business standpoint is that I'll cut someone's throat over money, and that cannot be further from the truth. I believe that people fall for this notion because I talk about wealth a lot. In this industry though, you are either a product person or a wealth person. I have just always been the guy that talks about wealth. There was definitely a point when it was all about my money; all about the next cycle and a time when the more money I made, the better I felt. That is not the case anymore. If it were true and that is what I am really about, then I would have stayed where I was at Zielar; sold everybody out, made a whole lot more money and went on with the ebbs and flows of business, but I didn't. Yes, I like money and helping others to create it, but I don't love it; there is a difference. I like what it provides— the ability to give back and help others. And honestly since the accident, even my promoting the wealth vs. the product has been more balanced. I am definitely more sensitive to (about) the products because, they gave me the ability to heal myself back up over the last eighteen months. There has to be a good balance, so that part of me has changed.

After I left Zielar in 2009, I struggled because you have to get into a good company. It is sort of like finding a great fit in a pair of shoes. They may come highly recommended, be made of great quality material, labeled by a renowned name and even feel good when you try them on, but once you take them home and try to work them for the long haul, they just aren't right. So, it took me a few tries to find the right company. Being at the level that I've attained, you are brought into a company and they tell you whatever they need to because they know that you can positively impact their company. And the opportunity looks good when people say certain things, but once I get in there and begin to work, the operation is different. As it pertains to *Network Marketing*, there is no bad choice, there are just some better than others. So the truth of the matter is that the right opportunity, the right vehicle had not presented itself to me for the direction in which, I wanted to go. By the release of this book however, I will be in the right opportunity. I know what it is, I'm going to run with it and I'm excited. In my heart, I believe it will be my last run and that it is a company that will be around forever. The owner is a gentleman around my age who understands the dynamics of what it takes to be successful. He himself used to be a distributor. His parents owned a company. I am absolutely looking forward to it. It is the first time in about six years that I have felt this confidant and I felt confident about Zielar, but I know, this is going to be bigger than Zielar.

Now I have reverted back to my roots; back to what I know is right, my mission is still Faith, Family and Prosperity— but in that order only; and to use my platform to bring people closer to *God*. I am more focused on giving back to my community. In the past, I've always given to my organization or people closest to me, but not necessarily to the whole community like I should. I would like to have a broader reach of people that I can impact from books, audio, radio shows, personal appearances, donating my time or resources— whatever I can do. I also want to positively impact the younger generation, especially the younger male population. Under the Cedric D. Penn Foundation, I look to create a program; "Mentor The Champions," teaching young boys how to become men. There is a lot that they can learn from my life and the subsequent lessons. I believe that they are a lost generation because there are not a lot of male mentors or role models out there for them to look up to. So, I think that it is my responsibility to do whatever is within my ability to be a part of the solution; reaching back to ensure that we do not leave them behind.

As I listen to others speak stories of their struggle and survival, I am able to empathize and say I understand what you are going through, I know how you feel. Often however, people do not believe me; discarding my sincerity. They perhaps, look at where I am in life today and think that there is no possible way for me to relate. My family and I have been through *hell* and back. I have lost everything but my *dignity* or my desire to be something. I would never allow anyone to take that away. Life is about pressing towards a mark, outwardly to accomplish personal goals, though ultimately to forge a deeper imprint, an in stone legacy to pass through your family. It is because of mine, whom have always stayed by my side, always supported me through every aspect of my life; the good and the bad, the thick and the thin, the reasons that I press forward; striving to do more, to be more, to continue the dynamic legacy passed down through *"Thunder"* and *"Big O"* Clemons. And though, as a family we may not always agree with each other's decisions, let us remain united in the teachings of Catherine Travis Penn *"Sergeant Carter"*, as we— too, continue her legacy. Know that I am there for you always, whenever you need anything. To my children and grandchildren— through the coming generations; take what my *Grandparents* started and continue the *Clemons* name. Stand for something and always give back. When adversity hits and the roads get rough, *lean* on tradition because that is when you need it. Tradition, Work Ethic, Goals *and*

Culture. With humility, hard work, dedication and commitment, drive your passion and stay focused following one course of action until successful. And remember, they don't have to like you, just make them respect you.

"I Will Continue To Do Whatever I Have To Do To Get What I Want. Until I Get My Family Where I Want Them To Be, I Will Until…."

BILL "ROMO" ROMANOWSKI

After 16 years in the NFL and 4 Super Bowl Championships, Bill Romanowski, the founder, President and CEO of Nutrition53 Inc., has dedicated his post football career to helping you achieve Optimal Life Performance. Optimal Life Performance is about you looking better, feeling better and sleeping better so you can live your best life.

Romanowski's passion for athletics and performance started at a young age of 14, when he was inspired by an article on strength and fitness from NFL legend, Running Back Herschel Walker. Walker's article outlined a simple but rigorous routine of push-ups, sit-ups, pull-ups, and nutrition of fresh fruits, lots of vegetables, and lean proteins. As one of five children in a family of modest income and a determination to seek higher education, Romanowski set his goals on earning a college scholarship through academics or athletics.

Romanowski followed Walker's guidelines religiously through high school with his site set firmly on his goals. His hard work, passion, and dedication were rewarded with numerous high-school accolades and eventually an athletic scholarship to Boston College. His work-ethic continued, and his coach at Boston College described him as "Possibly the best kid (he) ever had." While at Boston College, he helped the team win the 1985 Cotton Bowl as the Defensive MVP and he was later selected as the third finalist for the Dick Butkus Award for outstanding linebackers in college football.

He graduated with Academic Honors and a degree in Business Management. After graduation, Romanowski was drafted to the San Francisco 49ers where he teamed up with the likes of NFL legends Ronnie Lott, Jerry Rice, Joe Montana, and Roger Craig. The team won back-to-back Super Championships in 1989 and 90. Romanowski became one of only three players in NFL history to win back to back Super Bowls with two different organizations when he again won Super Bowl Championships in 1998 and 99 with the Denver Broncos. In his final Super Bowl trip in 2003 with the Oakland Raiders, he became the only Linebacker in NFL history to start in 5 Super Bowls Games. He retired from Football in 2003 after 16 years in the NFL, 5 Super Bowl Games, 4 Super Bowl Championships, 2 Pro Bowl Selections, and an NFL record of 243 consecutive games.

Romanowski attributes his success and longevity in the NFL to his rigorous training, pristine nutrition, and the support of his family, especially his wife Julie.

www.Nutrition53.com

Success Stories

"In business, of course, one should have a plan and priorities for their success. Prosperity was our goal however; having our priorities in the right order would be a key part to build a successful business along with having a more fulfilling life experience. Cedric Penn, more than anyone before or since, was able to drive home the importance of balance in our lives; pointing to Faith, Family, and Prosperity as key core values for the journey. Passion and enthusiasm are so important when you're looking for the motivation to build a lasting business, you have to feel these things and Cedric's passion and enthusiasm rub off on you. Focus and consistency, do a few simple things consistently over a period of time helping others build a strong foundation and equal longevity in *network marketing*. Focusing on core values and applying these important and basic principles have built a solid foundation for our current and future success, both with our family and most defiantly our business. Thank you Cedric!"

Allan and Cindy Chrenek are young professionals living in Calgary, Alberta, Canada. They have a young son, Olin, and attribute their early success, under Cedric's leadership, applying these principles to reaching their first goal to be able to stay home a raise their family.

"About three years ago my life was changed by Mr. Penn; he showed me that I had the power to be my own boss through systems. Today I am self-sufficient, achieving my own goals and dreams; not someone else's! I learned through the help Of Mr. Penn and the Diamond Network that I too had the ability to start my own company, AST International, LLC. Thank you Mr. Penn for sharing your life with us all, you are truly an inspiration!! See you at the top..."

Khatib Y.A. Ritter
Atlanta, Georgia

"On a personal level, Cedric Penn is made of the highest ethical fiber I know and has a deep understanding of friendship and family. I am honored that for the past 14 years I am able to call him one of my closest friends.

Cedric is the true embodiment of a mentor. Not only has Cedric shared with me the tools which have allowed me to create wealth, he has also shown me how to reinvent and implement positive thinking for my clients.

His ability to ignite anyone into action is remarkable, and if you are someone who wishes to attain a personal or business goal, then I highly recommend reading The Cedric Penn Story. His experiences of struggle and triumph are refreshing, extremely candid and inspiring. Be careful. Success leaves clues and you will find many in this book.

Thank you Cedric for not only sharing your story, but for also reminding us once again that we can achieve and create anything we want out of life."

Lonnie Robinson,
Washington, D.C.

For Additional Information Regarding

Cedric D. Penn

Media Inquiries and Booking Consideration Contact:

Monica Emery

(225) 802-6160

MonicaE@CedricDewaynePenn.com

For Information Regarding the

Cedric D. Penn Foundation

Contact:

Support@CedricDPennFoundation.org